D1630074

DEPRESSION AND PROTECTIONISM:
BRITAIN BETWEEN THE WARS

MODERN REVIVALS IN ECONOMICS
Series Editor: Professor Mark Blaug

Melvin L Greenhut
A Theory of the Firm in Economic Space
(0 7512 0074 3)

Hollis B Chenery and Paul G Clark
Interindustry Economics
(0 7512 0156 1)

Carl S Shoup
Ricardo on Taxation
(0 7512 0060 3)

John Creedy
Edgeworth and the Development of Neoclassical Economics
(0 7512 0109 X)

Dick Netzer
The Subsidized Muse: Public Support for the Arts in the United States
(0 7512 0142 1)

C D Throsby and G A Withers
The Economics of the Performing Arts
(0 7512 0174 X)

John Creedy
Dynamics of Income Distribution
(0 7512 0195 2)

William J Baumol and Wallace E Oates
Economics, Environmental Policy, and the Quality of Life
(0 7512 0108 1)

William J Baumol and William G Bowen
Performing Arts – The Economic Dilemma
(0 7512 0106 5)

Mark Casson
Unemployment: A Disequilibrium Approach
(0 7512 0216 9)

William J Baumol
Welfare Economics and the Theory of the State
(0 7512 0107 3)

Wallace E Oates
Fiscal Federalism
(0 7512 0220 7)

Ian M T Stewart
Reasoning and Method in Economics: An Introduction to Economic Methodology
(0 7512 0202 9)

Roy Harrod
Economic Dynamics
(0 7512 0211 8)

Alec Cairncross
Economics and Economic Policy
(0 7512 0227 4)

Kenneth K Kurihara (ed)
Post-Keynesian Economics
(0 7512 0246 0)

**Alvin H Hansen and
Richard V Clemence (eds)**
Reading in Business Cycles and National Income
(0 7512 0247 9)

Nicholas Kaldor
An Expenditure Tax
(0 7512 0249 5)

Harry G Johnson
Money, Trade and Economic Growth: Survey Lectures in Economic Theory
(0 7512 0250 9)

Tibor Scitovsky
Papers on Welfare and Growth
(0 7512 0251 7)

Tibor Scitovsky
Welfare and Competition
(0 7512 0253 3)

Alan T Peacock and Jack Wiseman
The Growth of Public Expenditure in the United Kingdom
(0 7512 0256 8)

**Giovanni A Caravale and
Domenico A Tosato**
Ricardo and the Theory of Value Distribution and Growth
(0 7512 0257 6)

Stefano Zamagni
Microeconomic Theory: An Introduction
(0 7512 0261 4)

Harry G Johnson
Essays in Monetary Economics
(0 7512 0259 2)

Harry G Johnson
Further Essays in Monetary Economics
(0 7512 0260 6)

Forrest Capie
Depression and Protectionism: Britain between the Wars
(0 7512 0262 2)

DEPRESSION AND PROTECTIONISM: BRITAIN BETWEEN THE WARS

Forrest Capie

Professor of Economic History,
City University, London

Gregg Revivals

First published in Great Britain in 1983 by
George Allen & Unwin (Publishers) Ltd

Reprinted by arrangement with Routledge in 1994 by

Gregg Revivals
Gower House
Croft Road
Aldershot
Hampshire GU11 3HR
England

Gregg Revivals
Distributed in the United States by
Ashgate Publishing Company
Old Post Road
Brookfield
Vermont 05036
USA

British Library Cataloguing in Publication Data

Capie, Forrest
  Depression and Protectionism: Britain
  Between the Wars. - New ed. - (Modern
  Revivals in Economics Series)
  I. Title II. Series
  330.941082

ISBN 0-7512-0262-2

Printed in Great Britain by
Ipswich Book Co. Ltd., Ipswich, Suffolk

Contents

Preface

My interest in the subject of protectionism derives from three sources. The first was working as a civil servant administering import controls and being concerned about the causes and consequences of these policies. The second was some research I did on protection in the agricultural sector in the 1930s. The third was the developing mood of protectionism in the mid 1970s. Much of this recent protectionist mood, and some emerging consequences, looked at least at first glance very similar to the 1920s and 1930s; and as the years have passed the similarities have increased. It therefore seemed worthwhile to examine that previous experience more thoroughly – particularly the economic origins and effects of the abandonment of free trade. A great deal of attention has been given to political aspects of the event but much less to strictly economic factors. These latter are then the focus of this study and it is hoped that the outcome is of value to the current debate on protection. In Bacon's words, 'it should excite the judgement briefly if not inform it tediously'. The book should appeal to the student of international economics and commercial policy and to the student of modern British and international economic history.

I have incurred many debts in the process of writing the book and I should like to thank several people. The research was funded in part by a grant from the Social Science Research Council. Rob Davies provided stimulating research assistance. David Harkess gave unstintingly of his expert computing guidance. Michael Collins listened patiently to the arguments and offered constructive criticism. Geoffrey Wood kindly read the whole manuscript. Barry Eichengreen and James Foreman-Peck made valuable comments at important points. Pamela Angel has done an admirable job of typing without complaint. My greatest debt however is to my wife Dianna, without whom none of the research would have been undertaken.

1

Introduction

Free trade is not the natural order, but something that has been struggled for and, once achieved, defended against the multifarious forces of protection. There have been two outstanding examples of success: the first was in the developing international economy in the third quarter of the nineteenth century, and the second was in the Western world in the third quarter of the twentieth century. Both were comparatively short-lived episodes. Writing of the American readoption of tariffs in the closing quarter of the nineteenth century, Jacob Viner talked of 'the end of the intermission in Mercantilism', and this idea, of a free trade interlude between long periods of state regulation of trading activity, is a much more accurate characterisation of the norm than the one held by many, particularly those unencumbered with heavy historical baggage. The common experience in international trading relations has been the erection of barriers to trade in the selfish and largely misguided pursuit of greater gain. Only in the period between the Second World War and the 1960s was there a broad-based concentrated effort at promoting free trade in the world economy. Actively avoiding the perils of protection was prompted by the calamitous trading experience of the 1930s. But in spite of the valiant attempts at trade liberalisation of post-1945 and a period of success, the international community is again sliding into protectionism and is more and more arranged in various trading blocs. Invisible barriers to trade have been growing and, in the 1970s and 1980s, protectionist forces and measures can be found emerging everywhere.

This book considers the case of the oldest advocate of free trade, and its greatest exponent, Britain, and examines the developments that led to the reversal of that policy in the 1930s; it also considers the consequences of the protectionist policy for the domestic economy. This introductory chapter provides some background, outlines the argument of the book and draws attention to some aspects of the problem that are either not dealt with explicitly or not dealt with at length.

The book concentrates on the domestic economy – on the pressures for protection arising there (or at least manifesting themselves there) and on domestic effects of tariffs – but this will be placed within the context of prevailing conditions in the international economy. When examining the domestic pressures for protection in Britain we shall note how war and economic instability in the 1920s produced conditions that facilitated the growth of protectionist forces. The international setting in that decade was complex, however, and the first task is to present a sketch of that setting.

Before the First World War there had been signs of a movement back to trade protection in many parts of the world – a reflection of the growth of nationalism. The First World War, itself a product of political and economic nationalism, exacerbated the spreading distrust and tensions nascent in 1913. In the 1920s this continued on a greater scale as new states were created. The gold standard was suspended in 1914 by all the belligerents. But when Britain abandoned the standard in a formal legal fashion in 1919, that signalled the beginning of several years of floating exchange rates, which, in the climate of the time, did nothing to promote confidence or any sense of cooperation. What was needed was some lead, and Britain was reluctant to assume (and partly incapable of assuming) such leadership and the United States had withdrawn into isolation, rejecting involvement in European affairs and remaining outside the League of Nations. The absence of cooperation is brought out in two areas. One was war debts: some countries, such as Britain, favoured writing them off while the United States insisted on repayment. More serious was the reparation burden imposed on Germany, this largely at the insistence of the French. These were of such a scale that, as Keynes pointed out at the time,[1] the Germans could never repay them, and the payments simply aggravated the international payments problem.

Economic stability depends in good part on political stability, and political stability in the years immediately after the First World War was to say the least fragile. Mussolini's march on Rome in late 1922 and the French invasion of the Ruhr in 1923 dealt further blows to a shaky structure. Depreciating currencies, in part the product of uncertainty and instability, were accompanied by soaring inflation, the latter being both cause and effect. Such was the climate of the international economy even in the middle of the 1920s. There was some establishment of order after that and some recovery in the major economies. But Britain's return to gold in 1925, and the subsequent readoption by others, was done in such an *ad hoc* fashion and at unsatisfactory rates that it contained all the seeds of its own destruction. When collapse did finally come in the financial crises and economic depression of the years 1929–32, a fresh outburst of protectionism appeared and world trade collapsed.

Trade flows had suffered quickly and severely in the war of 1914–18. Consumer goods production was replaced by military production; shipping was requisitioned for war; there were hazards of transporting goods around the world; all these led to a virtual cessation of normal international trade. Countries deprived of goods they had formerly imported were forced to produce substitutes and it was these infants established in wartime that were part cause of the protective legislation after the war. Of course on top of all this there were the huge material and human costs of the war (7 million died) and after the Armistice was signed the atmosphere in international relations was full of bitterness. The international economy was physically changed, for example by the total withdrawal of the Soviet Union, and it was psychologically changed by the whole range of factors that emanated from the bitter distrust.

Tariff barriers around the world grew in size and number after the First World War, many of them having their origins in that war.[2] Some were 'legitimate' in the sense that they protected infant industries, and there had been many infants born in wartime. Others can be attributed simply to the exuberance of nationalism. The birth of new states (a product of war and its resolution) contributed to the growth of nationalism and led to economic antagonisms that resulted in protection. Further, when one important country adopted protection, other countries were liable to follow for no good reason. Governments have seldom been attracted by the niceties of theoretical argument or convinced by the genuineness of an infant industry at such times, and were inclined simply to retaliate. The Fordney–McCumber tariff of 1922 and the Hawley–Smoot tariff of 1930 in the United States are widely regarded as having been unnecessary in any sense. They represented purely retaliatory, irresponsible action from such a major economy, and provoked in their turn further retaliation.

The need for revenue was an argument advanced by countries suffering from balance of payments deficits. Most primary producers enjoyed a brief boom immediately after the war but thereafter suffered from sluggish demand that was the result of the slowdown in population growth and relatively sluggish income growth in their important markets. They faced a severe fall in agricultural prices and a deterioration in their terms of trade and found themselves in deficit. Agricultural communities everywhere were badly affected and these were often powerful political groups. It is not going too far to say that the agricultural lobby in the United States was a major factor behind the growth of protection in that country in the 1920s. European countries were similarly affected and Britain was not excepted. British farmers were very vocal and played their part in supporting protection, claiming that it was cheap imported food that was destroying domestic agriculture. In spite of their claims being false, or at least greatly exaggerated, they had a considerable degree of success in a variety of measures that were adopted after 1930.

The principal international organisation of the time was the League of Nations. The League busied itself with the problem of protection – indeed was the international focus of such activity and worked to resist the protectionist pressures – but had little success. Restrictions on trade were widely condemned by almost all international bodies. They had been categorically condemned at the Brussels Financial Conference in 1920, at the Porto Rosa Conference of 1921, again at Genoa in 1922 and at the Geneva Conference on Customs Formalities in 1923. In 1924 a resolution on free trade was passed by the League that was well received by country delegations. At the World Economic Conference in 1927 it was the view of the League that 'there appears to be a sufficient consensus of opinion in favour of abolishing or reducing to a minimum the system of import and export prohibitions'.[3] The League's economic committee, investigating the problem at the time, believed that most countries accepted the principle of suppression of prohibitions, but that the time for international action was not quite ripe and would not be ripe until some monetary and economic equilibrium had been re-established. Although there was a deep resolve to attack the growth of customs tariffs, the preliminary draft agreement drawn up for the 1927 conference shows how out of touch the League was, for it talked of the abolition of all trade restrictions and prohibitions within six months and even of ridding the world of invisible barriers to trade. However, there was a let-out in that the final article of the draft agreement stated: 'Nothing in this Agreement shall affect the right of any contracting state to take. . . all necessary measures to meet extraordinary and abnormal circumstances and to protect the vital economic and financial interests of this State'.[4] By the time the final report of the conference was drawn up, a much more realistic position had been adopted.

On the one hand the League seemed aware of the insurmountable immediate obstacles and looked to a holding operation. And while the same high-sounding sentiments as had been expressed at previous conferences were present again, a practical scheme was also outlined. The League claimed it was the unanimous desire of the members of the conference to make sure that 1927 would mark the beginning of a new era 'during which international commerce will successively overcome all obstacles in its path that unduly hamper it'. Along with this there was a sensible proposal that, if agreed upon, would have led to a containment of tariffs and provided the basis for gradual elimination.[5] The scheme included the recommendation that all countries should sign and ratify the Brussels Convention of 1913, which provided for consistency of definition of traded goods. The report also realistically listed the steps that should be followed thereafter. There would be a unification of tariff nomenclature and a simplification of customs tariffs that would do away with double schedule tariffs (that is, where there was a maximum schedule designed for bargaining purposes and a lower schedule that was adjusted to the needs of the country).[6] The conclusion of an earlier study by the League showed that bargaining tariffs were a particularly poor device and even one of the direct causes of the high tariff rates that characterised the post First World War period.[7] Following a simplification of nominal tariff structures and a unification of nomenclature, stability of tariffs would then be made feasible and could be pursued with greater hope of success.

In the midst of all this there was an interesting British contribution that has been almost wholly neglected and, as a result, whose significance has never been determined. This was the work of a Conservative Member of Parliament, Sir Clive Morrison-Bell, who embarked on a one-man crusade to promote European cooperation in trade. His method was to demonstrate the futility of the obstacles to trade by building a physical model of the tariff walls of Europe. The model received enormous publicity all over the world. Photographs appeared in the local newspapers wherever the model was exhibited. A special pavilion was built to contain it at the World Economic Conference in Geneva in 1927 and it attracted great numbers there and wherever else it was shown. However, the argument of the model was not unambiguous. Some did not seem to know whether it was an argument for protection or free trade. The *Morning Post*, which was highly protectionist in outlook, exhibited 'Tariff Walls' in its window, and when asked for its return begged for the loan to be extended. This proved impossible since the Free Trade League in Manchester had booked it! In 1930, Conservative Office – promoting a protectionist line – wanted to use it in their political campaign. But the most notable example of its use in support of protection was in the United States. When Senator Smoot's attention was drawn to it he found in it a vindication of his protectionist views and decided it must go on show in the Senate building; it did and it stayed there to assist the passage of the Hawley–Smoot tariff bill in 1930. Smoot used it to show how dangerously protectionist Europe was and stressed the need for the USA to take similar action.[8]

The failure of the international campaign against tariffs, in so far as it can be so described, was a result of domestic forces overcoming international sentiment. As one writer put it; 'protectionists worked on the home front while the internationalists were encouraging each other abroad. No national government was strong enough to resist the political pressures of the minority interest groups.'[9]

All of the activity on the international front reflected the dominant academic view, at least in the English-speaking world, on international trade. Academic opinion in the interwar years was firmly of the view that free trade maximised welfare. The traditional case was argued on the grounds of efficient allocation of resources and that the restriction of imports led to a reduction of exports or increased the flow of capital abroad. Keynes was steadfastly in the mainstream of thought on this issue in the early 1920s when he said, 'is there anything a tariff can do that an earthquake could not do better?'. He also took the widely held position that protection certainly could not cure unemployment. It is true that by the end of the decade Keynes had moved away from the classical positon to a belief that the traditional free trade case did not hold when there were less than fully employed resources, and that he had moved to arguing for a revenue tariff that would help relieve the budgetary difficulties and revive business confidence. But he regarded this as an emergency measure only and one that would be dropped when world prices recovered. He rejected the idea as soon as the gold standard was abandoned in 1931, the pound depreciated and the need for a revenue tariff was rendered redundant.[10]

The purpose of this book is to place the British return to protection in this setting, showing that the protectionist forces were on the move from the First World War onwards. It will also draw attention to certain aspects of the subject that have been relatively neglected and thereby seek to improve our understanding of the economic origins of the industrial tariff in Britain. Using an explicit economic framework, it will also examine the determinants of the shape of the effective tariff structure, and take a new approach to a consideration of the effects of the tariff. The structure of the book is as follows. Chapter 2 lays out the path of British trade over the years 1900–39.

Ever since the second half of the nineteenth century there had been a growing concern in Britain with foreign industrial rivals, increasing competition in trade and the possibilities of a solution in Empire self-sufficiency. The promotion of Empire trade by various means became a declared objective, and this chapter provides essential background to the trends in trading relationships that date from the 1870s and to some of the reasons lying behind these trends, particularly those associated with Empire. The chapter also provides information on related issues such as trade balances. More importantly, it examines the changing pattern of British overseas trade over the years 1904–39 and discusses some prominent explanations for the Empire bias that entered into the pattern.

There are a number of useful histories of commercial policy that provide all the necessary detail on measures that were in force in the period and of the additional legislation that grew up. There is no point in reproducing a catalogue of tariff measures here and so Chapter 3 simply describes the measures briefly, providing essential information for the reader.[11]

There follows the first part of the argument on the origins of tariff legislation. Briefly this is that the emphasis should be shifted from viewing the tariff as a sudden, unpremeditated response to the world economic depression that began in mid-1929; rather it should be seen as being the outcome of a variety of economic causes that date essentially from the First World War and flourished in the 1920s. Primary sources are used in this part of the exercise in spite of a huge secondary literature on the political origins of the tariff. The reason for this is that the book is concerned primarily with the much neglected area of business involvement and responses to their pressures. Chapter 4 tackles the question of the tariff arising out of the crisis of economic depression. One point that can be made here is that the depression of 1929–32 in Britain was not as severe as is sometimes believed. Output fell in only one year, 1931, and that by 5.6 per cent. The trade balance was not seriously weakened before 1931 and yet by that date the tariff legislation was prepared and it was hastily introduced in November 1931 in the form of the Abnormal Importations Act. This chapter will show that that Act looks very much like an excuse, and a feeble one at that, for preparing the way for the general tariff.

Having shown that the tariff policy was not entirely, and possibly not even mainly, the result of depression, the way is open to show in Chapter 5 that the reversal of the free trade policy had as much to do with pressures originating in the First World War and developing with the economic difficulties throughout the 1920s. One of these pressures came from Empire. In particular, the protectionist Dominions had been extending tariff preferences to Britain from the 1890s onwards and had an interest in seeing Britain armed with protective measures that could be used to keep foreigners out, but at the same time pave the way for some preferential arrangements being made that would allow Empire countries easier access. This was a pressure that found a sympathetic hearing amongst some sectors of British industry, notably those with Empire markets. Against this there was the wider 'international' desire, already described, for freer trade. But in spite of the sentiments expressed at the many international conferences on the need to reduce tariffs, tariff walls continued to be raised in most industrial countries. Thus pressure on Britain also arose from the domestic fear that without tariffs Britain would become the dumping ground for manufactures facing prohibitive barriers elsewhere. An extension of this latter argument was that the barriers could then be employed as bargaining weapons in trade negotiations. One pressure group in particular is given extra attention, that of the Empire Industries Association, combining as it did an element of external pressure with a domestic one. The emphasis of this book is none the less on the way in which the pressure was manifest on the domestic front. As already remarked, international sentiments were laudable but it was what was happening in the domestic economy that really mattered. Some policy-makers and economists were of course alert to the fact that, in times of economic hardship, unless there exists a body of 'vigilant and informed opinion continuously active to resist the appeals of special interest for protective measures the tendency to impose them is very strong'.[12]

It is of course difficult to quantify the effect of such pressure on government policy, but some quantitative assessment is made of the forces that attempted to shape the tariff structure in Chapter 6. This is done within the framework of the type of politico-economic models that have been used on similar types of problems for the United States and Canadian economies.

Empirical assessment of the economic effects of the industrial tariff have always presented difficulties, and in the 1930s there were serious complicating factors in terms of fluctuating exchange rates and widespread economic uncertainty. At the time, very little serious investigation of the effects of the tariff was carried out, even among responsible sections of the academic and government communities. Unfortunately this has also proved true of economic historians, and too often the results of contemporary casual observation were simply carried into the economic histories of the period. The difficulties of investigation have not diminished with the passage of time but some advances in theory have allowed fresh approaches to the problem to be taken. Chapter 7 provides some economic historiography of the topic that illustrates this before using a conventional approach of elasticities and partial equilibrium analysis. But an important contribution of this book is to follow this with an alternative means of investigation, namely the use of 'effective' protection rates (Chapter 8). The development of the theory of effective protection came in the 1960s and 1970s and there have been a large number of empirical studies for the recent past.[13] There are, however, still relatively few treatments of historical episodes, which is a pity since that is where the challenging cases lie.[14] A principal objective of the calculation of effective rates is to indicate the likely impact of protection on the direction of resource flows in the economy; the effective tariff structure shows which industries would have benefited most and which least in this respect.

Having outlined the argument of the book, it may be helpful to draw attention to certain aspects of the tariff that are not dealt with. First, the book deals only with the *industrial* tariff and leaves aside other restrictions. One of the principal 'other restrictions' was quotas on foodstuffs and I have shown elsewhere that these were not of great importance since the degree of substitutability between the imported and the domestic product was not high – certainly nowhere near as high as the farming lobby successfully claimed.[15] Other protective measures such as export credit schemes and subsidies on production did exist but again, without being controversial, it can be fairly confidently asserted that their combined effects were rather small, certainly in relation to the industrial tariff. It was the industrial tariff that was at the centre of the stage both in the origins and in the effects of commercial policy in the interwar years, although some of the other measures were undoubtedly important in signifying to trading partners that the policy reversal was total, and of course the quotas on foodstuffs were used as a basis for giving imperial preference to some Empire countries.

Second, to repeat, the focus of the argument is on the domestic economy and, apart from the international context sketched above, further discussion of the international economy and pressures originating there is limited to the chapter on trade patterns, or to where it is otherwise implicit in the actions of the domestic producer. For example, the concern of British industrialists to safeguard their home market could not help but affect the international economy and so involved the responses of foreign producers and governments. Equally, where the concern of British industrialists was to avoid antagonising an overseas market they may well have opposed pressures for a British tariff or at least held back support for such moves. These international aspects are noted but it is rather the net effects of these forces that are dealt with even though the forces may have more distant origins.

Finally, in this introductory chapter, some reference should be made to political factors. It is, of course, impossible completely to disentangle the subject of protection from its political aspects. The great bulk of the writing on the subject of the industrial tariff has either been by political historians, or can be found in the memoirs of politicians and domestic and international civil servants, and more recently in the political biographies of some of the leading political figures. For example, at the party level the struggle within the Conservative Party in the early 1920s revolved around the issue of protection. The story of Baldwin's conversion to protection, or his adoption of protectionist outlook for political gain, and his injection of the issue into the electoral battle of 1923, meant that that general election was about one issue – protection. Equally, the struggle of the early 1930s within the National government between the free trade Liberals who suffered such torment over their association with protectionist Conservatives was an essentially political event. These aspects of the subject have been extensively treated. But whereas, for example, many economic historians now regard the repeal of the corn laws in the 1840s as an event of political, rather than economic, significance, the economic case for the 1930s has not been examined in sufficient depth, so that there are many who have never recognised anything other than the political side of the 1930s issue. Because the economic aspects have been relatively neglected, this study is of the *economic* origins and the economic effects of the industrial tariff and it does not deal explicitly with the political aspects of the origin and effects – at least not at any length. It is further argued that economic analysis can assist in some clarification of the issue, even where that is political, and make a contribution to our understanding of the nature of the origins of the change in policy.

Notes

1 John Maynard Keynes, *The Economic Consequences of the Peace* 1920), ch. V.
2 The following is an indication of nominal tariff levels in the 1920s:

	(1)	(2)	(3)	(4)
Austria	13.2	14.0	—	—
Belgium	10.0	10.0	8.5	—
Czechoslovakia	20.6	18.5	—	26.0
Denmark	7.0	9.0	—	—
France	14.0	16.5	12.5	—
Germany	14.2	15.5	10.0	16.0
Hungary	23.0	19.0	—	34.0
Italy	17.2	16.0	15.75	19.0
Netherlands	4.4	8.0	—	—
Poland	24.4	22.0	—	59.0
Spain	40.0	26.0	37.25	—
Sweden	12.8	13.0	12.25	—
Switzerland	11.2	11.5	—	—
United Kingdom	5.0	9.5	—	—
United States	34.0	—	32.0	—
India	—	—	10.5	—
Australia	—	—	9.75	—
South Africa	—	—	9.0	—
New Zealand	—	—	8.5	—

Sources: (1) Figures of Preparatory Commission, League of Nations, Geneva, 1925.
(2) Morrison-Bell estimates, *Morrison-Bell Papers* (House of Lords), 1925, vol. 1, p. 160.
(3) Estimated *ad val.* incidence of tariffs on British goods in 1924, Balfour Committee, *Report of the Committee on Industry and Trade (1926–30)*, London, HMSO, 1930.
(4) Layton-Rist estimates, *The Economist*, 1926.

3 League of Nations, *Abolition of Import and Export Prohibitions and Restrictions* (1927), Economic Committee.

4   ibid., Section III.
5   League of Nations, *World Economic Conference Final Report* (1927).
6   The French tariff of 1892 was an outstanding example of this.
7   W. T. Page, 'Memorandum on European Bargaining Tariffs', League of Nations (1927).
8   *Sir Clive Morrison-Bell Papers* (House of Lords). Morrison-Bell wrote a book with a fascinating record of these events entitled *Tariff Walls* (1930). A photograph of the model was estimated to have been reproduced in over 1500 newspapers.
9   J. B. Condliffe, *The Commerce of Nations* (1950).
10 Donald Winch, *Economics and Policy* (1969).
11 D. R. E. Abel, *A History of British Tariffs 1923–1942* (1945); E. B. McGuire, *The British Tariff System* (1951); NIESR, *Trade Regulations and Commercial Policy of the United Kingdom* (1943).
12 Lionel Robbins, *The Economic Basis of Class Conflict* (1939), p. 124.
13 W. M. Corden, *The Theory of Protection* (1971), cited the earliest examples of these.
14 One of the first examples was G. R. Hawke, 'The United States Tariff and Industrial Protection in the Late Nineteenth Century', *Economic History Review* (1974).
15 Forrest Capie, 'The British Market for Livestock Products' (PhD Thesis, 1973); Forrest Capie, 'Consumer Preference: The Demand for Meat in England and Wales 1920–38', *Bulletin of Economic Research* (1976).

2

The Changing Pattern of Trade, 1900–39

This chapter describes how, and suggests why, British trading patterns changed over the years 1904–38. Behind the exercise lies the question: did Britain successfully find relief from foreign competition by turning to the Empire (a declared policy, particularly after 1932), or did the commercial policies of 1932 (tariffs, with preferential rates for the Empire, and quotas) simply accelerate a longer-term trend – that is to say a drift in trade towards the Empire for other reasons – or did they change the pattern in some other way?

A hazard to avoid in a description of overseas trade is the simple recitation of the trade components (exports, imports, trade balances, etc.) and of their changing growth rates or market shares. What is needed is a framework that examines some questions on why trade changed as it did and some answers that satisfy within certain limits.

An Outline of British Trade

First it is necessary to draw the outlines of trade and explain the period chosen. A brief description of the period 1870–1914 is provided in order to pick up the broad trends of the late nineteenth century. The main emphasis, however, lies in the years 1904–39, covering thirty-five years of trade, albeit ones including the First World War and the collapse of world trade in the deep trade depression of 1929–32. But the later period does allow for greater precision since the British classification of trade by country proceeds uninterrupted from 1904 (when certain changes were made) to the end of the period.[1] I shall describe the magnitude and direction of trade flows and look at the changing sources of imports and destination of exports. The commodity pattern of trade is also briefly described. Finally, an examination of trade balances with other countries is made in order to highlight particular components within the general pattern of visible trade. (Associated with this is the question of pressure brought by Britain or exerted on it in trading negotiations.)

1870–1914

The pattern of British trade between 1820 and the 1860s was relatively stable, but between 1870 and 1914 the British Empire more than doubled in size and the character of trade changed. In area, the Empire increased from 4.485 million square miles to 11.1 million square miles; and its population almost doubled, growing from 202.3 million to 372.1 million people. The number of territories comprising the Empire rose from around forty-seven to around seventy-three (depending on the definition used).[2] *The Times* kept the public informed of this expansion with daily accounts of new territories acquired or extended. Of Mark Twain's comment on the process, 'And the meek shall inherit the earth', Lilian Knowles remarked that this 'was not regarded as a joke, but as a just appreciation of the situation rather remarkable in a foreigner'.[3]

Given the great growth of Empire territory, and the concomitant diminution of 'foreign' territories, it would be surprising if British trade with the Empire had not grown at a rapid rate and indeed if *ceteris paribus* there had not been some slowing down in 'foreign' trade. Certainly we should anticipate some shift in the statistics on trade away from foreign and towards the Empire, as a simple consequence of the definitional changes. Table 2.1 presents a guide to this, providing trade figures for Empire and foreign countries in aggregate at 1870 and 1914,[4] and Figure 2.1 provides a graph of the course of trade over the period in between. These figures give an indication of the changing size of trade values (in current prices). It can be seen that total British imports more than doubled but that

Table 2.1   *Distribution of British Overseas Trade, 1870 and 1914*

	1870		1914	
Imports from:	£m.	% share	£m.	% share
Foreign	238.4	78.6	508.8	73.0
Empire	64.4	21.4	187.8	27.0
Total	302.8	100.0	696.6	100.0
Exports to:				
Foreign	188.7	77.3	342.3[1]	65.1
Empire	55.4	22.7	183.9[1]	34.9
Total	244.1	100.0	526.2[1]	100.0

[1] Includes re-exports.
Sources: British Parliamentary Papers, 1872, vol. LXIII; 1916, vol. XXXII.

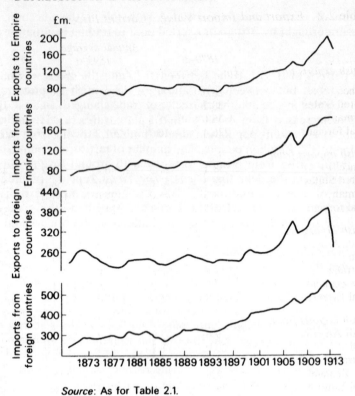

Source: As for Table 2.1.

Figure 2.1   British Trade with Empire and Foreign Countries, 1870–1914

those originating in the Empire almost trebled. Exports to the Empire had a roughly parallel course, more than trebling in value, while exports to foreign countries failed to double. This is shown up in the percentage shares these respective areas occupied in the total: while the Empire grew from almost 23 per cent to almost 35 per cent, foreign countries slipped back by more than 12 per cent.

The most important sources of British imports within the Empire in 1870 were, in order of importance: India, Australia, North American colonies and the West Indies. By 1914, the first three sources were still the most important, though North America had jumped to first place. The West Indies had fallen out of the leading group being replaced by Southern Africa and New Zealand. The three principal sources were also the main destinations for British exports in 1870; and again the West Indies was an important customer. In 1914, the five principal destinations for exports again included India, Australia and North America; added to these were Southern Africa and New

Table 2.2 *Export and Import Values (Current Prices)*

British exports to:	1870–3 £m.	% change	Annual average 1893–6 £m.	% change	1910–13 £m.
France	28.5	−29.1	20.2	49.7	36.8
United States	38.2	−6.5	35.7	69.8	60.6
Germany	36.6	−15.3	31.0	87.4	58.1
Total foreign	226.4	−10.7	202.2	196.8	400.1
British imports from:					
France	38.1	21.3	46.2	−3.7	44.5
United States	59.3	57.8	93.6	38.0	129.2
Germany	18.5	46.0	27.0	157.0	69.4
Total foreign	265.5	22.1	324.2	66.1	538.4
British exports to:					
North America	9.4	−22.3	7.3	+254.0	25.9
India	20.2	+44.1	29.1	+99.7	58.1
Australia	11.8	+34.6	15.9	+123.3	35.5
New Zealand	2.3	+65.2	3.8	+184.2	10.8
Total Empire	61.9	+30.9	81.0	+123.5	181.0
British imports from:					
North America	9.6	+45.8	14.0	+97.9	27.7
India	29.9	−11.7	26.4	+78.8	47.2
Australia	12.8	+78.9	22.9	+65.9	38.0
New Zealand	2.6	+215.4	8.2	+142.7	19.9
Total Empire	74.5	+25.6	93.6	+91.8	179.5

Source: As for Table 2.1.

Zealand. The other outstanding feature of these sources and destinations for imports and exports is the extent to which they dominated total Empire trade. In spite of there being over seventy territories in the Empire in 1914, over thirty of which were acquired in this period, these five areas alone took the overwhelming amount of British exports and supplied the great bulk of British imports from Empire sources – 80–85 per cent of all exports to and imports from the Empire.

World trade had enjoyed a great boom in the middle of the nineteenth century but after the 1860s the rate of growth slowed. Expressed in current prices and for the years 1883–1913 world trade grew at an average annual rate of 3.4 per cent. British exports slowed down considerably from the mid-Victorian boom years (1853–73), when they were running at a rate of 3.3 per cent per annum, to 1.6 per cent per annum for 1873–99. British imports, although also increasing less rapidly than in mid-century, continued at a rate greatly

Table 2.3   *Average Percentage Share of Various Countries in British Trade*

	1870–9	1880–9	1890–9	1900–9	1910–14
British exports to:					
Canada	3.2	3.3	2.6	3.4	4.5
Australia	5.3	7.3	6.2	5.6	6.6
India	8.5	11.0	10.2	10.2	10.9
New Zealand	1.3	1.3	1.4	1.8	2.0
France	10.2	8.7	7.2	6.5	6.7
Germany	12.1	9.9	10.7	10.2	9.7
United States	10.6	12.9	12.5	11.2	11.4
British imports from:					
Canada	2.9	2.8	3.6	4.4	4.0
Australia	4.3	5.0	5.1	4.5	5.3
India	8.2	8.6	6.5	5.9	6.5
New Zealand	1.0	1.4	1.9	2.4	2.9
France	11.6	10.0	10.9	8.7	6.0
Germany	5.8	6.3	6.2	7.4	9.1
United States	19.8	23.1	23.9	22.4	18.4

Source: As for Table 2.1.

in excess of exports (4.5 per cent per annum). Tables 2.2 and 2.3 are given in order to bring out the different experiences of leading Empire and leading foreign countries. These tables show very clearly that the principal Empire countries dragged the aggregate Empire figure up, and that three of Britain's most important foreign trading partners were performing less well than the rest of the foreign sector.

At the beginning of this period the principal commodities entering into the British import list from the main Empire sources were raw cotton, jute and indigo from India, wool from Australia and timber and wheat from North America. The West Indies supplied sugar. In 1914 most of these economies were less dependent on one or two export items and were supplying a greater range of goods, though almost all were still foodstuffs. India had lost the indigo market, since German synthetic dyestuffs proved too competitive. With the opening of the Suez Canal in 1869, bulkier cargoes developed, especially from India, which was the greatest beneficiary of the reduced freight rates. By 1913 wheat exports had more than compensated India for the loss of indigo, becoming her third most important export to Britain, next to tea and jute; raw cotton had slipped to fourth place. Australia, too, was exporting substantial quantities of wheat: it was her third most important export to Britain, next to wool and meat.

Dairy products were also becoming significant for Australia. Wheat was of course Canada's propriety by 1914, when she exported three times as much as either India or Australia; this expansion was primarily the result of the growing urban population of the United States diminishing the latter's exportable surplus. Canada also exported other important items to Britain such as cheese, timber, wheatmeal and flour and, interestingly, some manufactures. The West Indies supplied sugar and, although the trade continued to grow, it lost its relative importance. Southern Africa and New Zealand became important with the supply of wool and dual-product meat.

In the list of exports to these important Empire markets the items that dominated were cotton piece-goods, woollen and worsted goods, iron and steel manufactures and machinery. But standing out above all others in importance was the export of cotton piece-goods to the Indian market; indeed, cotton exports to India were worth more than all exports to the Canadian and New Zealand markets put together.

1904–1939

The essential elements of British overseas trade over the period 1904–39 can best be captured in similar graphical and tabular form. Table 2.4 gives the annual exports, imports and re-exports by value, together with a volume index for the period. The value figures are unadjusted, imports remaining in cif form and exports fob.[5] The table shows that, in value terms, total exports and re-exports had quadrupled between 1904 and 1920 and then collapsed by the end of the interwar period. Imports, on the other hand, held up much better. Much of this movement in values is, however, simply a reflection of the price movement, as we can see when we turn to the volume index. Here we find a less dramatic picture for exports and quite a different course for imports. Export volumes collapsed after 1930 and had not recovered their pre-First World War level by 1938, whereas import volumes in 1938 were far higher than they had been before the First World War.

Before 1904 British imports were classified as received from the country in which they were placed on board ship for export to the United Kingdom, and exports were given as distributed to the country to which they were shipped direct. So countries without seaboards were not distinguished. From 1904 onwards, particulars were collected on country of ultimate destination or country of original despatch. This change in the classification removes many of the previous obstacles to a clear picture, and provides the starting date for this examination.

Table 2.5 presents the main geographical features of Britain's export and import trade, by showing the six largest customers for exports and the eight largest import sources, which in aggregate

Table 2.4 *British Trade by Value and Volume, 1904–38*

Year	Value (£m.)			Volume (1938=100)		
	Exports fob	Re-exports fob	Imports cif	Exports	Re-exports	Imports
1904	301	70	551	114	127	66
1905	330	78	565	125	137	67
1906	376	85	608	135	138	69
1907	426	92	646	146	145	70
1908	377	80	593	134	134	68
1909	378	91	625	140	147	69
1910	430	104	678	152	150	71
1911	454	103	680	158	154	73
1912	487	112	775	167	165	78
1913	525	110	769	173	165	81
1914	431	96	697	NA	NA	NA
1915	385	99	852	NA	NA	NA
1916	506	98	949	NA	NA	NA
1917	527	70	1064	NA	NA	NA
1918	501	31	1316	NA	NA	NA
1919	799	165	1626	95	129	73
1920	1335	223	1933	123	148	92
1921	703	107	1086	86	129	60
1922	720	104	1003	119	133	70
1923	767	119	1096	129	141	77
1924	801	140	1277	132	159	86
1925	773	154	1321	130	155	89
1926	653	125	1241	117	135	93
1927	709	123	1218	134	141	96
1928	724	120	1196	137	137	93
1929	729	110	1221	141	132	99
1930	571	87	1044	115	126	96
1931	391	64	861	88	120	99
1932	365	51	702	88	106	86
1933	368	49	675	89	99	87
1934	396	51	731	95	99	92
1935	426	55	756	102	103	92
1936	441	61	848	104	102	99
1937	521	75	1028	113	106	105
1938	471	61	920	100	100	100

Sources: Value: *Annual Statement of Trade of the United Kingdom*, 1904–38; Volume: 1904–13, A. H. Imlah, *Economic Elements in the Pax Britannica* (1958); 1919–38, *LCES Bulletins*. Series have been linked to a common base.

Table 2.5   *Principal Sources and Destinations for British Imports and Exports (Average Percentage for Each Period)*

		Rank	1904–13	1920–9	1930–8
USA	M	1	19.55	19.99	11.96
	X	2=	6.73	6.79	5.06
	X&R		10.78	8.62	6.05
Germany	M	5=	9.39	3.77	4.57
	X	5	8.74	4.61	4.24
	X&R		10.36	6.63	5.70
France	M	5=	7.40	5.36	3.67
	X	4	5.89	6.24	5.38
	X&R		6.75	6.38	6.48
India	M	2	6.41	5.27	5.44
	X	1	12.28	12.28	8.57
	X&R		10.28	10.68	7.65
Australia	M	3	5.01	5.15	6.27
	X	2=	6.13	7.57	6.30
	X&R		5.61	6.89	5.69
Netherlands	M		—	—	—
	X	6	4.07	4.89	3.94
	X&R		4.31	4.93	3.95
Argentine	M	4	4.74	6.08	5.84
	X	NA	—	—	—
	X&R		—	—	—
New Zealand	M	8	2.64	3.85	5.02
	X	NA	—	—	—
	X&R		—	—	—
Canada	M	7	4.11	5.30	7.04
	X	NA	—	—	—
	X&R		—	—	—
Foreign	M		76.36	69.61	64.01
	X		65.31	57.30	53.52
	X&R		69.49	61.01	56.57
Empire	M		23.64	30.39	35.99
	X		34.69	42.70	46.58
	X&R		30.51	38.99	43.43

M – Imports
X – Exports
X&R – Exports and Re-exports
Sources: 1904–13: calculated from *British Parliamentary Papers*, 1916, vol. XXXII; 1920–38: calculated from *Annual Statement of Trade of the United Kingdom*, 1920–39.

Table 2.6 *Annual Growth Rates of Trade, 1904–38*

	1904–13	1922–9	1933–8	1904–38
UK–Empire	4.0	4.0	7.9	2.3
UK–foreign	3.3	3.6	4.5	0.6
Empire[1]–foreign	4.9	3.4	5.6	1.5
Intra–Empire[1]	4.4	1.6	9.3	2.3

[1] Excludes United Kingdom.
Sources: calculated from *Statistical Abstracts for British Empire* (various).

account for almost 50 per cent of United Kingdom overseas trade. If we look at the Empire–foreign (that is imports and exports from and to Empire and foreign areas) distribution first, we find that as the period progressed more and more imports came from the Empire and reciprocally less from foreign sources. Almost exactly the same pattern is observed for exports, though at a slightly lower level; that is, whereas in the early twentieth century an average of 34.7 per cent of British exports went to the Empire, by the 1920s that share had risen to 42.7 per cent and it rose further in the 1930s to 46.6 per cent. What we undoubtedly see is an accelerating movement in exports away from 'foreign' trade towards Empire trade. It is interesting that some writers have suggested, when looking only at the 1920s and 1930s and discovering this movement, that the Ottawa Conference of 1932 and the growing penchant for swapping tariff preferences were responsible for this shift.[6] What this table suggests is something quite different – that this movement was part of a much longer trend in overseas trade.

Some further light can be thrown on this by looking at Table 2.6, where annual growth rates of trade for various combinations of British, Empire and foreign trade within the period 1904–38 are given. In the early years of the century, UK–Empire trade in total was growing faster than UK–foreign trade; this was still true of the 1920s, though the difference had narrowed. But then in the 1930s a much faster growth rate was achieved in UK–Empire trade. The most remarkable growth of all, however, was between Empire countries (excluding Britain) in the period 1933–8. Empire–foreign trade was growing rapidly in this period, too, but the suggestion implicit in this table is that Empire trade, however viewed, was growing at faster rates than trade with or amongst foreign countries – and there is a noticeable increase in this rate in the years following Ottawa. All types of Empire trade grew at their fastest rates by a long way in the 1930s.

The commodity pattern of British trade was fairly stable throughout the interwar years, in that there were few shifts (and these not

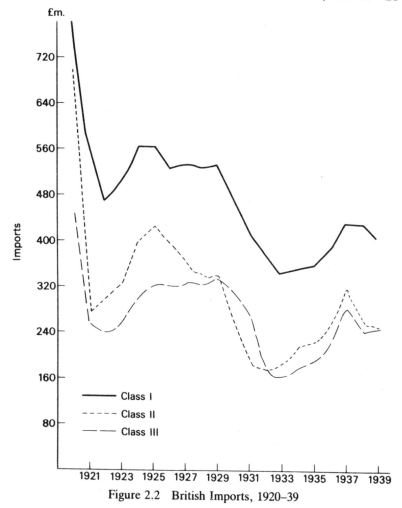

Figure 2.2   British Imports, 1920–39

large) in the relative size of the various commodity groups traded. Figure 2.2 presents the annual values of imports by major class (in current prices) and it is clear from this that total imports in each class exhibited a distinct cyclical pattern. The vertical line at April 1932 indicates when the general tariff was introduced. (When the price effect is removed the same peaks and troughs remain but the dramatic cycle is taken out of imports. For exports a pronounced cycle remains in the constant price series.) Class I (food, drink and tobacco) was always the largest import group. Class II (raw materials) and Class III (manufactures) took second and third places respectively, except for the years of the great depression when their positions were reversed. All three classes experienced more or less the same pattern of peaks and troughs, with raw materials exhibiting a substantial lead over manufactures only in the great depression. Classes IV and V (not shown here) are made up of a variety of miscellaneous items but are too trivial to warrant discussion. Ignoring the extreme value for the very unusual year of 1920, and again talking in terms of current prices, the highest and lowest import values for the period (1924/5 and 1932/3 respectively) moved through the range of £1300m. to £700m. Class I moved from £560m. to £350m., raw materials from £400m. to £160m. and manufactures from £320m. to £140m. At the disaggregated level of commodity groups within Classes II and III, some variation in pattern is observed but this is never great. Raw cotton, wool, wood and oil seeds are the four most inportant groups in Class II, while non-metal products, oil products, iron and steel manufactures and miscellaneous manufactures are the leading ones in Class III. The individual variation in the most important series can be seen in Table A.2 in the Appendix.

It is well known now that Britain has traditionally had a visible trade deficit that was more than compensated for within the current account by invisible earnings, principally from shipping (before the age of aircraft) and insurance. But of course the trade balance was not in deficit with every single country. Indeed, there were quite large surpluses with some countries. In the first half of the twentieth century there were some well-established triangular patterns of settlement; one of these was the UK deficit with the USA, which was partly offset by surpluses with tropical countries – chiefly India.[7] Table 2.7 presents the principal surplus and deficit countries (the gap in the middle of the table indicates that all other countries lie between these values, i.e. with relatively small surpluses or deficits). The largest deficit by a very long way throughout the entire period was that run with the United States. At the other extreme, the two largest surplus countries were South Africa and India. There are some interesting changes of position between the pre-First World War period and the interwar period. France, for example, moved from being third largest deficit country to third largest surplus country. The Netherlands, on the other hand, moved from a small surplus to a very substantial deficit. Another feature is that the 'New World' figures strongly in the deficit region. The fact that there was a reasonably large change between these two periods is confirmed by a rank correlation coefficient of 0.677 – in spite of the United States, India and South Africa keeping their traditional positions. Finally, Table 2.8 groups all trading partners, according to the sign on the trade balance, into positive, negative or mixed.

Table 2.7   *Mean Trade Balances for Principal Deficits and Surpluses, 1904–38*

1904–13		1920–38	
Country	*£'000s*	*Country*	*£'000s*
USA	−71,325	USA	−127,122
Russia	−17,018	Argentina	−40,008
France	−13,469	Canada	− 32,742
Denmark	−13,415	Denmark	− 28,858
Argentine	−12,466	New Zealand	− 26,565
North Africa	−9,874	Russia	−24,486
Germany	−9,536	Netherlands	−17,662
Spain	−8,560	Australia	−14,291
New Zealand	−7,943	Spain	−8,954
Canada	−6,450	North Africa	−6,795
Australia	−4,350		
		Germany	1,746
Netherlands	194	Italy	2,550
Italy	6,818	China	3,383
China	7,150	Japan	3,678
Japan	7,530	France	3,774
India	9,926	India	13,383
Southern Africa	10,896	Southern Africa	14,318

Source: calculated from *Annual Statements of Trade of the United Kingdom.*

Factors Influencing the Swing to the Empire

The tables in the first part of this chapter serve as background to an examination of the changing pattern of trade. An important feature of the geographical pattern of trade was a movement towards the Empire. This is of special interest in a study of the industrial tariff because Empire and protection and imperial preference were all inextricably bound up in the late nineteenth and early twentieth centuries. The question then that this section deals with is the relative importance of the forces that are said to have brought about the swing to Empire over the years 1904–38.

Although we are interested primarily in the years after 1904, it is necessary to pick up the story in the late nineteenth century. At that time foreign industrial and trading rivals turned to protection, while the white Dominions (also protectionist) extended preferences to the UK. At the same time, imperial visionaries such as Joseph Chamberlain were working diligently for closer trading links with the Empire. How important were these forces? Was there something in the nature of the commodities traded that steered Britain towards Empire

Table 2.8   *Trends in Country Trade Balances, 1904–38*

	Negative	Positive	Mixed
a.	*Empire:*		
	Australia[2]	India	North Africa[4]
	New Zealand	Southern Africa	
	Canada	West Africa[2]	
	East Africa	Other British possessions	
b.	*Foreign:*		
	Switzerland	China	Austria
	Czechoslovakia[1]	Portugal	Rumania
	Poland[1]	Greece	Hungary[1]
	Denmark	Bulgaria	Germany
	Russia	Turkey	France
	Sweden	Yugoslavia	Japan
	Norway[2]	Italy[2]	
	Netherlands[2]		
	Belgium		
	Spain		
	USA		
	Central America[2]		
	Argentine		
	Latin America		
	Rest of world[3]		

[1] 1921–38 only.
[2] with few isolated exceptions.
[3] positive for 1905–13.
[4] positive for 1915–22.

markets or did the First World War bring about changed trading conditions? Was it the sterling connection that influenced trade flows, or possibly exploitation of colonial territories? Or was it rather the growth of industrialisation and national income that determined trade? Had it anything to do with geography, as some recent writers would suggest? There are few unambiguous answers to these questions but some of them can be dismissed quite quickly either because it does not seem possible to reach any judgement on them or because the judgement is that they were not very significant. It should be clear that income was of primary importance (though this has still not been tested) but before looking at that more closely it will be useful to say something about some of the other explanations.

Empire Sentiment
When competition from trading rivals intensified some time after 1870 and protective barriers grew up, a movement for 'Fair Trade'

developed in Britain, which in turn gave birth to the Tariff Reform campaign. Both of these had inextricably bound up in them a desire for Empire trade. For some this was rationalised as a duty to the Empire; for others it was simple protection. The economic historians Cunningham and Ashley provided academic respectability for the movement in their writings.[8] Although the movement may have intially foundered with the electorate, certain actions were taken to promote Empire trade. Chief among the tariff reformers was Joseph Chamberlain who, as Secretary to the Colonies for the eight years 1895–1903, turned his considerable energy to promoting Empire unity. He believed the Empire might be self-sustaining:

> I will speak of its variety and of the fact that here we have an Empire which with decent organisation and consolidation might be absolutely self-sustaining.... There is no article of your food, there is no raw material of your trade, there is no necessity of your lives, no luxury of your existence which cannot be produced some-where or other in the British Empire.[9]

The impetus that Chamberlain gave is of course impossible to quantify, but the general feeling that through the Empire lay commercial salvation was very prevalent. There were the obvious 'natural' advantages of ease of communication in language (though the United States and some others would have been in a similar position). Commercial intelligence was more easily come by – though again perhaps not significantly more so, since skilful and diligent consuls in all parts of the world were by this time reporting back to the Board of Trade. Trading links were strengthened through the imperial conferences that date from the late nineteenth century and the establishment of imperial trade commissioners; postage rates were cheaper within the Empire; preferences were granted in the matter of loans on the part of Britain (which in turn, it was argued, facilitated spending on British goods by the Empire); income tax concessions were granted on money invested within the Empire; and there was a common approximation of various branches of commercial and industrial law. As the Dominions Commission put it:

> So long as freight rates are cheaper, and means of communication better, between the Mother country and the Dominions overseas, and between the Dominions themselves than between foreign countries and the Dominions, so long will trade naturally follow Imperial Channels.[10]

The simple concept of using the Empire as a form of relief from international trading competition is captured in the words of Baden-Powell:

It has been said that in Africa two thirds of the natives are unclothed and one third half clothed and that it is England's mission to clothe the half clothed and half clothe the unclothed. Even a rough statistical estimate of the number of yards of grey shirtings and other mysterious cloths of commerce needed for such a purpose would far and away outrun the capacities of all the mills of Lancashire and India combined. It has also been said that if these many millions or even any large proportion of them could be prevailed upon to wear flannel next the skin Australian squatters no less than Bradford manufacturers would have unprecedented cause for rejoicing.[11]

Of course it was partly a response to foreign tariffs that motivated this desired move towards Empire. The important industrial and trading rivals of Great Britain had been turning increasingly to protection after 1870. Germany led the way out of what Viner has called the 'intermission in Mercantilism' with a tariff in 1878, which she later extended in 1903. The Americans followed with the McKinley tariff of 1890 and the Dingley tariff of 1897. The French, too, imposed tariffs in 1892. It has been claimed that these tariffs led to the exclusion of British goods and, while such a claim may be exaggerated, there can be no doubt that the protectionist measures generated a mood that was conducive to seeking relief in Empire markets. By 1910 the average *ad valorem* rates of duty on *all* imports for the major European countries was as follows:[12]

Germany	8.4%
France	8.0%
Italy	9.6%
Spain	13.4%
Russia	38.9%

By the mid 1920s the corresponding figures were of the following order:[13]

Germany	15%
France	16%
Italy	16%
Spain	30%

Averages of nominal tariff levels are notoriously poor guides to the degree of protection and the extent of the exclusion of goods. Individual tariff rates coupled with price elasticities of supply and demand need to be known before anything can be said about the precise effects of these tariffs. However, it would seem reasonable to conclude that the return to protection on the part of these countries certainly contributed to British *concern* over trade and probably encouraged seeking out Empire markets where preferences at least were available. For example, in the 1880s British markets for leather goods were said to be restricted by German and American tariffs. German tanners enjoyed a 10 per cent protection from 1874 to 1906 and at the turn of the century the Americans were sheltered by a 20 per cent duty. German imports from Britain fell while German exports rose. Studies are still wanting for the 1920s, though an interesting one of the Fordney–McCumber tariff of 1922[14] concludes that it is doubtful whether any reduction of that tariff would have increased the flow of imports into the USA: 'Owing largely to non-tariff factors, it has been argued, the United States was self-sufficient in most of the export products from other industrial countries and from the temperate agricultural regions.'[15] Japan too was protection-ist. In 1914 certain consumer goods were subjected to duties as high as 40–50 per cent *ad val*. In 1926, when the tariff was revised, 'new industries' were protected. It should be said, though, that in Allen's opinion the tariff was not very important in Japan before 1920 and that in the 1920s exchange fluctuations were more important.[16] Nevertheless, foreign tariffs probably helped push Britain towards the Empire, though by how much it is impossible to say.

Capital Flows

Of the large numbers of other explanatory factors influencing trading patterns, capital flows were of importance before 1914. The flow of capital was, according to Lenin, a great source of exploitation, though the view that capital flowed more to Europe and the white Dominions by the turn of the century has been largely discredited by empirical work on the direction of capital flows. Nevertheless, as Saul[17] says, they did have much to do with the shaping of trade patterns at that time. By the late nineteenth century that role was greatly diminished.

Sterling Balances

Sterling balances may also have made it easier and more convenient for certain countries to trade with the UK. The sterling area was never rigidly defined, especially in the early part of the twentieth century, but there were two fundamental characteristics of 'member' countries: the first was that the bulk of their foreign exchange hold-ings were held in London; and the second was that the exchange rate between members' domestic currency and sterling remained fixed. Within this definition sub-divisions can be made between indepen-dent countries, rigidly dependent countries and those in a state of transition. This has not been tested explicitly in terms of balances held in London, for want of data, but to some extent it will be covered in the following discussion on exploitation/dependency.

Exploitation

A definition of economic exploitation is difficult, but Drummond has suggested the following: the existence of markets so arranged that buyers pay more than they would otherwise have paid or where sellers obtain less than they would otherwise have done.[18] Using this definition, Drummond concludes that there was little if any exploitation in British–Empire trade. Cartel arrangements may have led to some exploitation, but on the other hand the 'natives' were not very important buyers of the goods traded in the twentieth century (sophisticated chemicals, heavy machinery, etc.). The most obvious exploitative device would have been a tariff on Empire foods with the incidence pushed back on the producers; yet to a large extent free entry was preserved for Empire foods in Britain. There were tea and sugar duties and so on but usually with large preferences. Where any exploitation did take place it was hardly significant: 'However large the surpluses this extracted . . . it cannot conceivably have been large relative to the inter-war rise in British consumption.'[19]

Some earlier empirical work on this topic was that by Hirschman on the preferences that large trading countries had for trading with small (defined in terms of their trade) or weak countries.[20] Here the notion of exploitation is implicit – the suggestion is that it is easier for a large country to exert monopoly power and to force the weak country to be dependent on it. Hirschman produced an index that measured the extent of that preference:

$$\left[R = \frac{UA}{WA} \, 100 \right]^2$$

When the index is 100 the relative distribution of trade as between large and small countries shows no distortion. Where the index is less than 100 the hypothesis is nullified, and where over 100, the hypothesis is supported. The greater it is, the greater is the degree of preference of that country for trading with small countries. The index was calculated for major countries for the years 1913 and 1925–38. For 'England', the value for exports was always over 100 but nevertheless always lower than Germany and invariably lower than Italy. For imports, 'England' was again always over 100 but again usually lower than Germany, the United States and Italy. It is obvious that large trading nations are likely to trade with small trading nations (there being more of the latter), so there appears to have been very little marked preference on Britain's part for trading with small or weak countries.

When Hirschman reverses the process and seeks a measure of the concentration upon markets and supply sources of the small or weak countries, he uses an index whose range is 0–100. When a country's trade is completely monopolised by another, the value is 100. Hirschman finds that for countries in the British Empire both import and export indices were high compared with smaller European or Scandinavian or even South American countries. Typical values for the white Dominions' imports and exports were around 50. India's was lower while that of Nigeria was higher. An index figure of the same kind was calculated for 'England', which effectively provided the lower bound of the index – being very low at 20 and indicating a very wide spread of trade.

There is some secondary value in this measure for us, in seeing how these indices moved over time and in noting any difference of behaviour between 1913 and 1938. When we compare 1937 with 1913, we find that export indices maintained their high level whereas import indices decreased significantly. The result was brought about in two stages: 1913–29 and 1929–38. The first period shows a general decrease in both import and export indices (suggesting less monopolisation of trade taking place), while the second period shows import indices stationary but export indices rising significantly. The upward trend is most in evidence between 1929 and 1932, that is before the Ottawa agreements could have made themselves felt. It is Hirschman's conclusion that it was rather the depression, with its new trade barriers, that foiled the previously noticeable tendency for the countries of the British Empire to develop new markets.

Hirschman's general conclusion is that the association between country concentration and commodity concentration is positive and that 'world trade is built rather in large proportions upon the reliance of the export products of one particular country upon the prosperity and tastes of another individual country'. New Zealand butter in England, Philippine sugar in the USA and Bulgarian tobacco in Germany are examples of this. However, none of Hirschman's results helps very much with the question of dependence and exploitation.

More recently the problem has been posed explicitly and examined for some post Second World War years.[21] Kleiman's study focuses on the bilateral trade bias introduced by colonial rule. The argument is that colonial countries are said to trade to a greater extent with their metropolitan countries than they would otherwise do. Kleiman demonstrates that this is the case for the years 1960–2 by comparing the share of colonies' trade taken by metropolitan countries.

I tested this hypothesis for the British Empire for selected years before the Second World War. The share of Britain as the metropolitan country in the trade of the Empire is shown in Table 2.9. For the hypothesis to hold, the commodity trade of dependent territories would

Table 2.9 *Metropolitan Country's Share in Trade: UK–Empire*

	Exports			Imports		
	1913	1929	1938	1913	1929	1938
Canada	49.8	25.3	39.1	21.3	15.1	17.5
Australia	45.4	38.1	56.2	52.3	39.7	42.1
New Zealand	84.1	75.0	84.7	61.1	46.1	47.8
Southern Africa	78.8	48.4	38.8	56.7	43.9	43.9
India	23.4	21.3	34.1	65.4	43.8	31.3
East Africa	28.7[1]	39.3	38.0	28.3	28.5	19.3
West Africa	47.4	34.9	47.4	69.3	60.1	55.9
British Asia	36.7[2]	19.3	16.3	22.3	17.0	15.3
British South America	27.5	26.8	48.3	37.2	30.7	35.1

[1] Aden missing.
[2] North Borneo, Brunei, Sarawak missing.
Sources: calculated from *Statistical Abstracts for British Empire* (various).

be heavily concentrated in Britain, but an examination of the results hardly bears this out. For each of the years 1913, 1929 and 1938 New Zealand is the country that exhibits the greatest dependency on the British market. New Zealand sent 84 per cent of her exports to Britain in 1913 and while that had fallen to 75 per cent in 1929 it rose again to 84 per cent in 1938. Australia, Canada and South Africa also sent larger shares of their exports to Britain than India, East Africa, British Asia or British South America. There may be some individual countries within these broad groupings where the ratios were higher but overall there seems little evidence here for the exploitation thesis. When we look at imports, which is perhaps more appropriate to the test, we do find that West Africa took a larger share of her imports from the UK than any other part of the Empire but not much more than New Zealand. Again there is no unambiguous evidence here that supports the exploitation thesis.

Kleiman's measure of what he calls the 'degree of enforced bilateralism' is what he regarded as the excess of the metropolitan country's trade share over what might be expected in the absence of colonial rule. He used as a control group the metropolitan country's share in the trade of all other 'less developed countries'. This test was not used here for two reasons. One is that it is obvious that enforced bilateralism did not operate with the white Dominions, and the assumption is therefore spurious. The second is that, because of Britain's large slice of world trade before the Second World War, such a comparison is not helpful. In short, the conclusion is that there may have been a degree of coercion in trading relationships between the imperial power and the member country, but there is little evidence from the trade shares that it was extensive.

Imperial Preference

Even if there was little exploitation, the imperial connection may have been important via imperial preference. This factor would have been particularly important in the 1930s – that is, after the Empire Conference held at Ottawa in 1932, when Britain granted fairly substantial preference to Empire countries. The United States alleged that British preference was responsible for damaging US exports to Britain in the 1930s and preference became one of the bargaining issues in the UK–US Trade Treaty of 1938. The Americans felt so strongly about it that in 1942, as part of a deal on lend-lease, Britain agreed to end imperial preference. Some contemporary commentators in the United Kingdom also believed that preference was of considerable benefit to British trade in the 1930s. In a somewhat premature study, Sir George Schuster claimed that the Ottawa preferential arrangements had been responsible for increasing trade within the Empire and decreasing trade with foreigners – it was 'obvious that imperial preferences have played an important part in bringing about the shift'.[22] Hancock too, writing in 1942,[23] believed that imperial preference was certainly responsible for foreign traders suffering and British countries benefiting on trade, though the extent of that benefit was never measured.

Glickman was one of the first to publish the findings of a serious investigation into preference.[24] He examined the trade statistics for the years 1930–8 and found a changing direction that he attributed to imperial preference. There is an element of the *post hoc ergo propter hoc* here, for he does not examine other possible factors. However, even on this limited basis, his conclusions are that Britain did not gain in the white Dominions or other Empire markets, whereas the Dominions (notably Canada and Australia) gained greatly in the British market.

A more rigorous study was that of MacDougall and Hutt.[25] They ignored Glickman's contribution when they took the years 1929 and 1937 as the basis for their investigation. Their study calculates the average level of preference granted and received by the UK and the Dominions and other intra-Empire arrangements. These calculations show that the UK–Empire trade had average margins of preference of between 10 and 12 per cent in both directions by 1937. This was a fairly large increase over 1929 when Britain extended an average preference of 2–3 per cent on all imports from British countries and gained an average of 5 per cent on all exports to the Commonwealth. But the impact has to be considered small, for as we shall see later even the tariff had a small impact.

Both these studies have their uses, but both suffer somewhat from ignoring longer-term secular shifts that were taking place and the fact that some items enjoying preference may reap the rewards while others do not. If, for example, A extends a preference to B, B gains if it gets a higher price or sells more. If B produces more than A needs and therefore sells to C, the price is set in free conditions and B will not benefit. For these reasons, Meyer[26] concludes that the West Indies and others benefited from sugar preferences, Rhodesia from tobacco preference and Cyprus from wine preferences, but tea, coffee and cocoa producers did not gain.

Geography

Another factor has recently been advanced as an important determinant of international trade – that is, that trade tends to take place between neighbours rather than with distant cousins.[27] 'A near neighbour is better than a distant cousin' goes a well-known saying – apparently! 'Neighbour' has been carefully defined in some of the literature to mean having a common border, and distant cousin is taken to mean having special economic or political relationships. But a common border is not necessary and the degree of trade is alleged to be quite closely related to distance from market or source. Now, on the face of it, the idea that trade is some function of distance is a perfectly plausible hypothesis if not an overly exciting one, but when we turn to the experience of the British Empire in the first half of the twentieth century it is obviously not going to hold. Indeed, the opposite is more likely. The largest trading partners tended to be furthest away. In 1938, Australia was the biggest customer and could hardly be further away. The other large partners were India, Southern Africa, New Zealand, Argentina and so on. In order to introduce a little rigour into the refutation of the hypothesis, however, the calculation of a simple rank correlation coefficient was made to measure the association between the magnitude of Britain's exports to a market and the distance of that market from Britain.

Twenty-one countries representing the great bulk of British trade were selected and the calculation performed for three years over the period: 1913, 1929 and 1938. Obviously some difficulties arise, particularly with close European countries, over what distance to use. How far away is France? Should we take the London–Paris distance or the south coast–Bordeaux? In a ranking of distances, this difficulty is in fact minimised since all we have to say is that country A is closer than country B. The rank correlation coefficients were $-.324$, $-.373$ and $-.424$ respectively for these years. In other words, there was an inverse relationship between trade flows over distance which was more true as the period progressed. To put it another way, there is a weak connection between distance and degree of commerce for Britain and her trading partners in the first half of the twentieth century, and it is the opposite of what the geography hypothesis claims. That may not be remarkable, but it is worth making the point.

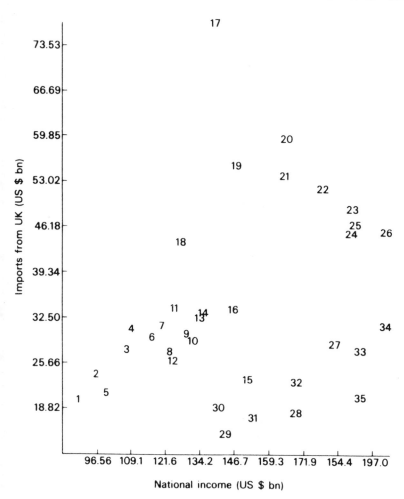

Figure 2.3a   Imports and Income of Selected Countries, 1904–38 (USA)

Income

I mentioned earlier that the growth of trade is widely held to be principally determined by the growth of income, more rigorously defined as GNP per head. It would seem obvious that trade would take place with richer, or most rapidly industrialising countries, yet on the face of it there is an apparent contradiction here since British trade with foreign countries was declining whereas that with the Empire was growing. The Empire was primarily non-industrial, a source of raw materials and foodstuffs, and 'foreign' countries were

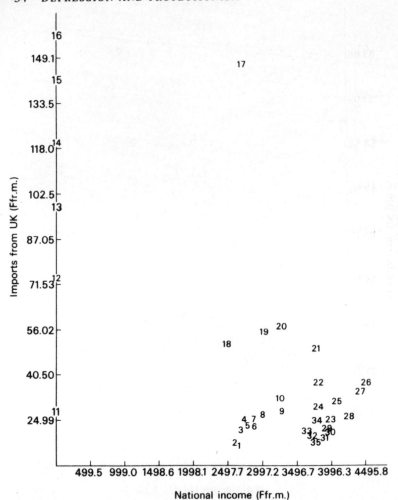

Figure 2.3b   Imports and Income of Selected Countries, 1904–38 (France)

principally Europe and the United States and therefore industrial. But while it may be tempting to see in this shift from foreign to Empire a contradiction of the general principle that industrial countries trade more with each other than with non-industrial countries, this would be incautious. When we look behind the aggregates we do find that trade with the United States was greatly in decline in spite of the fact that, over the first thirty years of the twentieth century, industrialisation there proceeded at a pace possibly unequalled elsewhere. And while there appears to be some further evidence of

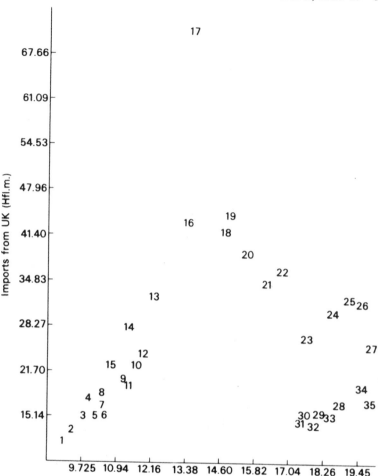

Figure 2.3c   Imports and Income of Selected Countries, 1904–38 (Netherlands)

contradiction in that British trade with France and Germany was falling off while that with Australia and New Zealand was increasing, the fact is that the white Dominions in the Empire were industrialising rapidly, while several industrial countries suffered from various problems between the wars.

In fact no close relationship between trade and income holds between the wars. A scatter diagram for the income of selected countries together with their imports of British goods is given in

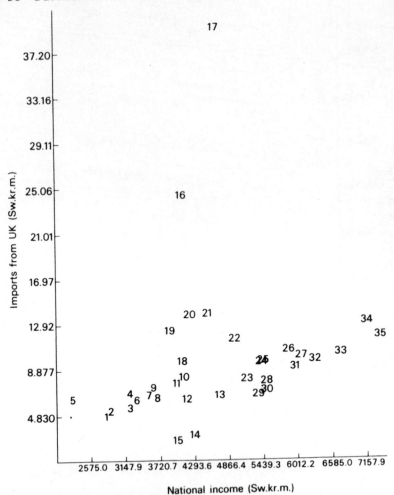

Figure 2.3d   Imports and Income of Selected Countries, 1904–38 (Sweden)

Figure 2.3. Table 2.10 shows that, for the period 1904–13, there is a very close correlation between income and imports of UK goods for the countries for which data were most readily available (France, Germany, Italy, Holland, Norway, Sweden, Spain, USA and Australia). A correlation coefficient in excess of 0.8 was obtained for almost all countries. For the interwar years, however, the relationship disappears, the coefficient in almost every case being negative. The only country where the relationship continued to hold was Australia where it was still moderately strong at .674. Obviously the role of

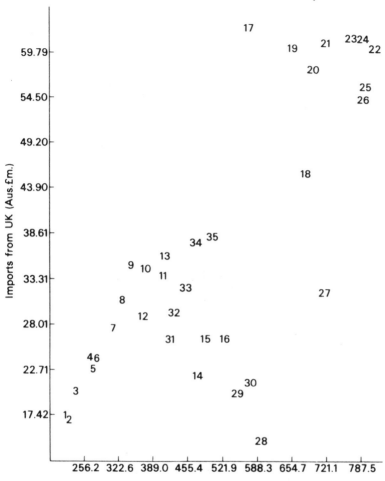

Figure 2.3e   Imports and Income of Selected Countries, 1904–38 (Australia)

income requires much closer and more rigorous investigation, but on the evidence here it was not the powerful determinant of trade between the wars that it has been at other times.

The First World War
Finally, the First World War deserves mention, though in terms of its lasting impact on trading patterns it was not as potent a source of change as it was in other areas of economic and social life. The

Table 2.10 *Income/UK Imports Correlation*

	1904–14	1920–38
France	.89	−.64
Germany	.81	−.27
Italy	.82	−.72
Holland	.92	−.74
Norway	.91	−.36
Spain	.56	.46
Sweden	.66	−.22
USA	.79	−.08
Australia	.99	.67

patterns in existence in 1904–13 were broadly taken up again after the disruption in wartime. For example, Australia, New Zealand and Argentina declined in importance as sources of meat products for the UK in 1914–18 and were replaced by the United States and Canada supplying pig meats in place of lamb, mutton and beef. But this did not last, and after 1920 there was a complete reversion to the pre-1914 pattern.

Notes

1 J. Stafford, J. M. Maton, M. Venning, ch. 14 of R. G. D. Allen, *International Trade Statistics* (1953), p. 293.
2 *British Parliamentary Papers*, 1872, vol. LXIII, Accounts and Papers, 28, No. 1; 1916, vol. LXXII, Accounts and Papers, No. 3; 1914–16, vol. LXV.
3 L. C. A. Knowles, *Industrial and Commercial Revolutions in Great Britain during the Nineteenth Century* (1926).
4 No distortion is introduced by taking these years singly rather than, say, five-year averages for the beginning and end of the period.
5 A balance of payments figure would require the conversion of cif to fob and many commentators have done this by deducting 10 per cent from the former, this being considered 'reasonable'. I have not for two reasons. The first is that 10 per cent may be a useful rough and ready guide and justified in its use when a transfer is being made within the balance of payments. But in our period, when carriage costs and freight rates changed considerably and when there was some decline in visible earnings, there seems little point in making an arbitrary adjustment.
6 Sir George Schuster, 'Empire Trade before and after Ottawa', *The Economist* (3 November 1934).
7 A. J. Brown, 'The Present Pattern of World Trade', *Banking and Foreign Trade* (1952), p. 25.
8 W. Cunningham, *The Case Against Free Trade* (1911); W. J. Ashley, *The Tariff Problem* (1903).
9 C. W. Boyd (ed.), *Chamberlain's Speeches* (1914).
10 *British Parliamentary Papers*, 1917, *Dominions Commission*, Cd. 8642.
11 Sir George Baden-Powell, 'The Development of Tropical Africa', *Proceedings Royal Col. Institute* (1895–6).

12 S. B. Clough and C. W. Cole, *An Economic History of Europe* (1968), p. 611.
13 C. W. Morrison-Bell, *Tariff Walls* (London, 1930).
14 M. E. Falkus, 'United States Economic Policy and the "Dollar Gap" of the 1920s', *Economic History Review*, (1971).
15 ibid., p. 622.
16 G. C. Allen, *A Short Economic History of Modern Japan* (1972), p. 129.
17 S. B. Saul, *Studies in British Overseas Trade 1870–1914* (1960).
18 Ian M. Drummond, *Imperial Economic Policy 1917–1939* (1974).
19 ibid., p. 445.
20 Albert O. Hirschman, *National Power and the Structure of Foreign Trade* (1945).
21 Ephraim Kleiman, 'Trade and the Decline of Colonialism', *Economic Journal* (1976).
22 Schuster, op. cit.
23 W. K. Hancock, *Survey of British Commonwealth Affairs, Vol. II Problems of Economic Policy 1918–1939*, Pt 2 (1942), p. 309.
24 David L. Glickman, 'The British Imperial Preference System', *Quarterly Journal of Economics* (1947).
25 Sir Donald MacDougall and Rosemary Hutt, 'Imperial Preference: A Quantitative Analysis', *Economic Journal* (1954).
26 F. V. Meyer, *Britain's Colonies in World Trade* (1948).
27 Hans Linnemann, 'Trade Flows and Geographical Distance, or the Importance of being Neighbours', in H. Bos (ed.), *Towards Balanced International Growth* (1969).

3

Tariff Legislation

The first policy movement away from free trade in Britain in the twentieth century might be said to have come in 1913 when the government granted a subsidy to the sugar beet industry. The first import duties, however, were those imposed by the Chancellor of the Exchequer, McKenna, in 1915. These duties were alleged to be emergency measures of wartime, renewable annually during the war, and for revenue purposes primarily. (The saving of valuable shipping space was also put forward as a reason.) But by normal definition and accepted practice the duties must be regarded as protective since there were no parallel excise duties; and they lasted long after the war, being still in force, apart from a brief lapse in 1924, in 1938 when they were finally incorporated into the general tariff provisions. The McKenna duties, as they came to be called, were levied at a rate of 33⅓ per cent *ad valorem* on certain luxury items: motor cars, clocks and watches, musical instruments, and a specific duty placed on cinematograph film.

Immediately after the war there was some movement away from import restrictions. There had been an attempt at counteracting 'dumping' or providing against the potential threat from 'dumping' in the form of the Imports and Exports Regulation Bill of 1919, but this was withdrawn. However, there was also a growing protectionist group that resisted any such drift and worked for the opposing cause. Their first success came with an indirect measure – the export credits scheme of 1919. This was ostensibly designed to stimulate exports to countries with unfavourable exchange rates, but it in fact provided protection for British producers by enabling them to defer the necessity of payment for a period of years. Ideas on safeguarding were first formulated at the Paris Conference of 1916 and were designed to meet a situation that might arise if Germany were not decisively beaten in battle. After the war, those seeking protection were able to use the idea successfully to secure duties in spite of the original requirement having disappeared.

The first measure to extend protection through duties was the

Dyestuffs Act of 1920, which provided for duties on a range of chemicals. Like much of the feeling of the protectionist movement, it was prompted by a desire 'to close the British market to German competition'.[1] The Safeguarding of Industries Act, 1921, placed duties of 33⅓ per cent *ad valorem* on 6,500 items of goods believed to be of strategic importance, goods such as scientific instruments, glass-ware, wireless valves, ignition magnetos, hosiery latch needles and so on. On optical glass the duty was 50 per cent. The legislation was limited to five years, this being thought sufficient time to allow the industries to become competitive. In fact the legislation was renewed for a further five years in 1926. At the same time the range of goods was extended in 1926 and at subsequent dates. Part II of the Act was concerned with special 'key industries' and the problem of dumping, particularly that arising from countries allowing their currencies to depreciate. There was a rush of applicants to secure protection under these provisions, but of 24 applications in the first five months not one was granted.[2]

Labour was the party of free trade in the 1920s and on gaining power in 1924 repealed the McKenna legislation and allowed some safeguarding duties to lapse. But Labour was in power for less than one year and the return of the Conservative government saw the restoration of the McKenna duties in 1925, the introduction of the Merchandise Marks Act and the imposition of a complicated set of differential duties on silk goods. In the period 1926–9 the safeguard-ing duties were extended to packing and wrapping paper (1926), items of pottery (1927) and buttons and enamelled hollow-ware (1928). In 1929, with a Labour government once more in power, some safeguarding duties were allowed to lapse and the anti-dumping provisions of Part II of the Safeguarding Act were repealed in the Finance Act of 1930. The measures that had been taken in the 1920s were all rather insignificant in terms of the volume of imports they affected but they were of some importance for their inroads on free trade ideology.

The 1930s witnessed the greatest changes in British commercial policy. In November 1931 the Abnormal Importations Act was passed, which allowed for duties of up to 100 per cent on certain items, though in fact the maximum imposed was 50 per cent. Three orders were made in considerable haste, imposing duties of 50 per cent on several items. The principal goods covered by the First Order of 25 November 1931 were pottery, sanitary ware, tiles, domestic glassware, metal furniture, cutlery, typewriters, woollen manufac-tures and linen goods. The Second Order of the same month added glass bottles and jars, woollen cloth and metal utensils. The Third Order of 19 December added a few others including cotton manufac-tures, cameras, wireless components, electric lamps. This Act was supplemented by the Horticultural Products (Emergency Duties) Act, which provided for duties on flowers, fruit and vegetables. The principal tariff legislation, though, was the Import Duties Act of February 1932. This imposed a 10 per cent tariff on all goods except those specifically exempted (the primary produce of Empire countries and most other food and raw material items). This general tariff was amended over the next few years through the recommendations made to Parliament by the Import Duties Advisory Committee, but most of the major revisions had taken place by the end of 1932. The first set of recommendations came in April 1932 and consisted primarily of the doubling of the nominal rate to 20 per cent on all items other than a few specifically left out. By the end of the year, most manufactured and semi-manufactured goods carried a tariff of 20 per cent and a few $33\frac{1}{3}$ per cent. In the iron and steel industry, for example, a duty of $33\frac{1}{3}$ per cent was passed on pig iron, 'semis', girders and sheets (in other words, on much of the raw material for the industry) and 20 per cent was levied on the main range of finished goods. As Benham remarked, 'for perhaps the first time in British tariff history a higher duty had been put on the raw material than on the finished product'.[3] One moderately important, but short-lived, change came in 1935, when the tariff on iron and steel was raised to 50 per cent to force the European cartel to come to an agreement on the quota to be imported into Britain. The success of the bargaining allowed for a reversion to the original level within a matter of months.

At the beginning of the 1930s, several other measures of a protectionist kind were also introduced. The abandonment of the gold standard in September 1931 and the depreciation of sterling against gold bloc currencies supported the protectionist case. Quotas were also popular. As we have noted, by the mid 1930s they were being negotiated on iron and steel, but they were more common on agricultural products – notably meat – from both Empire and foreign sources. In fact, in 1936 a tariff was placed on foreign meat entering Britain.

Several factors offset these protectionist devices, some exogenous, some not. For example, many important trading partners tied their currencies to sterling and thus avoided the potential disadvantage of appreciating against sterling. Of possibly equal significance was imperial preference. The cause of the Empire had been intimately bound up with the cause of protection for a long time. Since the end of the nineteenth century, imperial preference had been granted to Britain by the protectionist white Dominions, which had in turn sought some preferential arrangements in the British market. Britain first extended preference through the Finance Act of 1919, which allowed for reduced rates of duty on certain goods already subject to

Table 3.1 *The General Tariff on Paper*

		Preferential rate %	Full rate %
(1)	Paper (other than paper included in the next succeeding paragraph) and board made from paper or pulp, whether coated or otherwise treated in any manner or not (other than newsprint as defined in The First Schedule to the Import Duties Act, 1932), of a weight when fully extended equivalent to not more than 90lbs to the ream of 480 sheets of double crown measuring 30 inches by 20 inches, but not including (a) paper imported solely for the purpose of being spun into yarn.	10	20
(1a)	Tissue paper, and writing paper on sheets measuring not less than ... etc.	$6\frac{2}{3}$	$16\frac{2}{3}$
(2)	Paper, and board made from paper or pulp whether coated or otherwise treated ... etc.		
	(i) Kraft board imported in reels	5	15
	(ii) Other kinds	10	20
(3)	Articles ... made either entirely from paper or board ... etc.	10	20
(3a)	Boards consisting of a middle layer of thin strips of wood covered on both sides with a layer of paper or paper board	5	15
(3b)	Cigarette papers ...	$6\frac{2}{3}$	$16\frac{2}{3}$
(4)	Transparent cellulose wrapping	10	20
(5)	The following manufactures, whether coated or otherwise treated in any manner ...		
	(i) Kraft paper and machine glazed paper ... etc.	$6\frac{2}{3}$	$16\frac{2}{3}$
	(ii) Imitation kraft paper, greaseproof paper ... etc.	15	25
(6)	Periodicals bearing a reference to the time of issue thereof, if imported in a consignment of more than thirteen copies ... etc.		
	(a) ...		1s 0d per lb
	(b) ...		1s 0d per lb

duty where these were produced in the British Empire. The reduction was one-sixth the duty on most articles and one-third on McKenna goods. In the 1925 Finance Act there were several extensions, chiefly by virtue of new duties on cutlery, gloves and gas mantles. There followed over the next few years several minor amendments to these arrangements partly as a result of new duties or of the abolition of a duty, as in the case of tea in 1929. When the general tariff was introduced in 1932, preference was apparently greatly extended since it operated on almost all goods, the preferential rate being 10 per cent below whatever the full rate was. However, the Empire produced very little that qualified for such a preference, the chief exception being motor cars from Canada. Another action that deserves mention as offsetting to some extent protectionist measures was the revaluation of sterling in 1925 at a level generally believed to be around 10 per cent above its equilibrium rate. Lastly, the other large change that took place in commercial policy in the 1930s was the breakdown of the operation of the 'most-favoured-nation' principle and the substitution of bilateral agreements. Britain signed many such agreements, many of them providing for the actual bilateral balancing of trade with the specified country.

Any precise summary of the nominal tariff structure of the general tariff of 1932 is impossible, in spite of the apparent simplicity conveyed when rates are quoted. In detail it was quite complicated. There were sixteen groups within Class III (manufactured and semi-manufactured goods) in the *Trade Accounts*, and many of these groups required several pages to describe the application of the tariff. One of the simpler ones was Paper (Class III, Group XIII) but the condensed summary in Table 3.1, which shows eight different rates applying to various difficult-to-define sub-groups, suggests some of the difficulties that are encountered. Where the nominal tariffs are shown later, it should be remembered that they are an approximation taking into account the dominant items in a group.

A rough guide can, however, be given to the extent of the coverage of the tariff before 1931 and after. In 1930 almost 85 per cent of Britain's imports entered free of duty. By the time of major revisions in the tariff in April 1932 only 30 per cent of imports entered free of duty, a further 33 per cent were subject to duties of 10 per cent, around 15 per cent had duties of 11–20 per cent and something like 5 per cent of goods paid duties in excess of 20 per cent. After the refinements of the Ottawa agreements on August 1932, fewer goods were free of duties and slightly more paid the higher rates.

Notes

1   W. J. Reader, *Imperial Chemical Industries* (1970), p. 329.
2   R. K. Snyder, *The Tariff Problem in Great Britain 1918–1923* (1944), Ch. VI.
3   F. C. C. Benham, *Great Britain Under Protection* (1941), p. 178.

4

Depression and Protection

'What's the name of this queer place?' John asked.
'It's Tariff-land', said the White Rabbit, 'and it isn't a queer place, it's very beautiful.'
'But why has it got high walls all round?' John wanted to know.
'Oh!' said the White Rabbit eagerly, 'that's Mr. Joseph's new invention. It's to stop Dumping, you know.'
'Dumping! What is that?' John asked.
'It's a lot of nasty, horrid foreigners trying to sell us things we want cheaper than we want to pay for them', said the White Rabbit.

'And what's in that bag?' said John [of the Knight] pointing to what looked like a very heavy bag slung on to the saddle.
'It's full of 'arf-a-bricks,' said the Knight.
'What are they for?' said John.
'Why, to heave at the foreigners, of course,' said the Knight, much surprised at John's not knowing such a simple thing as that.
[Charles Geake and F. Carruthers Gould, *John Bull's Adventures in the Fiscal Wonderland*, 1904, pp. 17–18, 81]

The general tariff of 1932 has frequently been characterised as a policy of crisis, hurriedly devised and implemented to help cope with the economic depression of 1929–32,[1] but as this chapter and the next will argue the protectionist tide was well under way by 1929. There had been constant rumblings since the late nineteenth century about unfair competition in the British market, and clamouring by some for protective devices, but the protectionist movement gained greatest impetus during the First World War and found continuing support in the postwar world. The main pressure in the decade after the war came from the iron and steel industry; just as in the 1870s a turning point came with Bismarck's imposition of duties on iron and steel, so this industry was to play a major (if not necessarily the decisive) part in the British return to commercial protection in the 1930s. Thus the implementation of the protectionist policy should be seen more as the culmination of over a decade of pressure by interested parties, which built up to produce a powerful force when worsening economic conditions developed at the end of the 1920s.[2]

This chapter tackles the view that it was the depression that was responsible for the British abandonment of free trade. The argument is on two fronts. First the question of dumping is dealt with, for it was claimed by some that it was this unfair practice that finally left Britain with no alternative but to adopt protectionist measures. Secondly, an associated matter was the claimed flood of 'abnormal' imports in to Britain in late 1931, which led to the introduction of the Abnormal Importations Act of November 1931, a measure that helped pave the way for the general tariff legislation in early 1932. Chapter 5 will examine the protectionist pressure that built up from the time of the First World War and reached a climax in 1930–1.

Dumping

It is worth examining the idea that dumping was taking place in the British market in the 1920s on a threatening scale, for some contemporaries were persuaded that this had been influential in the return to protection. Thomas Rush of the National Federation of Iron and Steel Manufacturers writing soon after all the legislation was passed, said:

> The policy of continental manufacturers of dumping their products on this market at whatever prices they would fetch *finally* convinced the National Government of the necessity for Protection.[3]

Dumping is now, and was then, both a term of art and a term of abuse. It was a common catchword for 'unfair competition', but it was also accepted that there was a strict and potentially useful definition that covered the difference between the selling prices in the domestic and foreign markets. Corden, drawing on both Viner and Haberler, has provided a useful summary of the analysis of different types of dumping.[4] It may be private or public, short-term or long-term. Private long-term dumping arises out of the profit-maximising policies of a discriminating monopolist. If domestic demand is less price-elastic than foreign demand, dumping can result. No monopolist would export for a long period below the marginal cost of production, but public (that is subsidised) dumping takes place where an export subsidy is granted and the export price is then able to fall below the marginal cost of production. Short-term dumping can be of two types: sporadic or predatory. Sporadic dumping takes place when the foreign supply price falls, say for reasons of fluctuating demand. Or it may simply be the unloading of remainders at the end of the season. Either way it increases the risks to the domestic import-competing producer, though there are obvious benefits to the consumers. Predatory dumping occurs when a dominant foreign supplier temporarily reduces his price to force out a domestic producer. This is difficult to identify and will only be effective if the foreign exporter is able to sustain a monopoly. Haberler maintains that it was seldom found because of the high cost and the considerable risk of failure – arising for example from sudden legislation in the receiving country after a period of gains from the cheap imports.

There is still the question whether dumping is in the interests of the dumping country and against the interests of the receiving country? The private monopolist in the exporting country may make gains, indeed invariably does, but his fellow countrymen pay a high price in terms of the welfare losses of monopoly. For the receiving country, the lower the import price the better the terms of trade and the greater the possibility of a favourable trade balance. But this holds only so long as the improvement in the terms of trade is not temporary and the benefits are not lost to monopoly prices later. Given the importance of iron and steel as an input for British industry we might have expected much of the business community to have favoured 'dumping'. Indeed, Haberler quotes Palmer, president of the large shipbuilding company carrying his name, as saying, 'Let them sell at cut prices so long as they can. We shipbuilders are only too pleased.'[5]

The necessary conditions for dumping are that protection and monopoly should be present – that is, goods must be prevented from returning to the exporting country and a monopoly must obtain in that country. Some of these conditions do appear to have been present in the two countries most commonly accused of the practice – America and Germany – in the 1920s. In the case of Germany there may be something in the claim that for the years immediately after the First World War German dumping was carried out in order to compel other powers to recognise Germany's economic problems and provide an international loan to help the defeated nation back on its feet.[6] After 1921, talk of dumping within Germany seems to have evaporated. Haberler, writing in 1936, talks of German dumping of iron and steel in England, 'At a price often 50 per cent below the German price', but while he seems to be referring to the recent past he does not say exactly when, and he may simply have been using their earlier experience as an illustration.[7] No such extravagant claim appears to have been made by the British producer, at least not before 1930.

Trying to prove the existence of dumping has always been exceedingly difficult. While there was anti-dumping legislation on the statute book in Britain in the 1920s, only nine applications for duties were ever made.[8] Two of these got as far as the Board of Trade committee of inquiry, and duties on glass bottles and vulcanised tyres were the only duties imposed.[9] No duties were imposed on iron and steel goods, that important group of products, suggesting that dumping was not in fact the problem it was supposed to have been for that industry. The legislation was repealed in the Finance Act of 1930.

By the 1930s, allegations of dumping were common and feelings ran high. Evidence to the Civil Research Committee on Iron and Steel (1928/9) was frequently of the kind: 'with continental dumping our industry is doomed'. Mr Dixon of the forgings and coatings section of the National Federation of Iron and Steel Manufacturers (NFISM) claimed that it was impossible to compete against continental dumping; that the Germans were supplying forgings on the Clyde at £15 10s 0d per rough ton turned. He asserted, 'this is a dumped price'.[10] Mr Pugh of the Iron and Steel Trades Confederation (which was one of the few unions that supported their employers in seeking protection) was asked if the industry had suffered from dumping. He replied: 'there is no doubt a lot has been imported – the facts would tend to show that this was dumped in the sense that price did not express the real cost of production in the country of origin. We have had a good deal of that in the last eight years.'[11] The NFISM produced figures purporting to show that continental steel was sold for export at prices below country of origin prices. They claimed that in February 1931 US wire was offered cif at Glasgow at prices much below the same wire in Pittsburgh. And the following month they claimed that wire rods were quoted fob Antwerp at £5 12s 6d per ton, whereas bright wire drawn from the rods was only £5 0s 0d (in other words the wire was being dumped).[12] The evidence was never very convincing, however, and the iron and steel industry got no protection under the Abnormal Importations Act, 1931, an Act more or less tailormade for such a contingency.

Dumping cannot be proved, and should not be inferred, from simple observation of import levels, although high levels (in quantity terms) are nevertheless implicitly suggested in the allegations made at the time. In fact, however, the *volume* of iron and steel imports shows no great increase in the period. Since the beginning of the century annual imports had always been in excess of 1 million tons; in 1912 and 1913 they exceeded 2 million tons. In the 1920s they were usually slightly above that level, reaching a dramatic but unusual high of 4.4 million tons in 1927, which was undoubtedly attributable to decreased domestic output as a result of the previous year's coal strike. In 1930, 1931 and 1932 the figures were 2.9 million, 2.8 million and 1.6 million tons respectively. There is nothing in these figures to suggest large-scale importing.

To sum up, there are poor theoretical grounds for believing that dumping would have taken place in Britain at this time. Long-term dumping below the cost production was unlikely given the risks attaching to it in the climate of the time, and there is little reason to suppose that public dumping was widespread. The most important qualification would appear to be short-term dumping (either sporadic or predatory) with the uncertainty it creates. In the 1920s there was the additional emotive argument of the need to keep a vital industry healthy for fear of war, which in the circumstances should not be too lightly dismissed. The empirical evidence of widespread dumping of goods in Britain in the 1920s appears weak and it is therefore unlikely that this was the reason for the introduction of the general tariff. Rather, fear of the practice and belief that it was current were so widespread that it was a stimulus to the introduction of some barrier to imports.

Abnormal Imports

Those who hold the view that the return to protection was a crisis measure frequently point to the passing of the Abnormal Importations Act of November 1931 as an illustration of the nature of the import crisis and of the necessity of taking immediate and drastic action. Some point to the fact that the Conservative-dominated National Government insisted that the measure was a necessary expedient to protect the British producer from a flood of imports. For example, in a biography of Neville Chamberlain, MacLeod stated:

> First came the emergency tariff provided by the Abnormal Importations Act, which safeguarded the position while the Government was working out its permanent policy and gave immediate protection against dumping.[13]

A recent political history of the period perpetuates this story and accepts that the Act was needed while a permanent policy was worked out.[14]

Before examining these 'abnormal' imports more closely, it may be as well to consider the mood of the years 1929–31. The anti-free trade movement had been gaining momentum in Britain as well as in the rest of the world for some time. Attention in the mid and late 1920s was often focused on the high tariff walls in Europe,[15] and when this was followed by the imposition of the Hawley–Smoot tariff in the USA in 1930, it contrived to support the hardening feeling amongst Conservatives that it was time Britain introduced protective tariffs. Free traders were resisting, but with diminishing success. In the middle of 1930 the publisher Longmans approached the liberal economist and director of the London School of Economics, William Beveridge, with a view to a book that would help to 'combat the protectionist tide': 'it is evident that the country is about to be agitated by a propaganda on behalf of Protection', wrote Potter of Longmans to Beveridge.[16] And later that year the Liberal politician Samuel urged Beveridge to say something before the book came out: ' . . . the protectionist tide is proceeding unchecked . . . issue a brief statement . . . help stop the rot.'[17]

As early as 1929 Neville Chamberlain had written of 'my plan . . . to make tariffs or customs duties only a part of larger Imperial trade policy'.[18] Amery describes how the framing of a detailed tariff scheme was left to a committee of the Conservative Research Office under Cunliffe-Lister in late 1930.[19] As Beer notes, a 'complete tariff scheme was worked out in the early months of 1931, ready to be rushed through Parliament at a moment's notice'.[20]

By August 1930 the Associated Chambers of Commerce had adopted a report in favour of safeguarding and in October 1930 the Federation of British Industries found that 96 per cent of its constituent bodies supported protection.[21] At the same time, the Trades Union Congress was convinced that protection was the right course: 'We must have protection of our industries . . . That doctrine is fully accepted by the T.U.C. which last September at Nottingham approved the Report of the Economic Committee. . .'[22]

By mid-1931, support for protection was coming from all sides. The 1922 Committee was completely in favour of a tariff. Apart from the fanatically committed, there were many recent converts. Sir John Simon favoured an emergency tariff: '. . . is there any alternative but to insist upon putting at once some block in the way of the flow of free imports?'[23] Runciman (in an about-face from the year before when he had chided Lord Melchett for reneging on his free trade position), like a number of others at the time, declared:

> I have been a Free Trader all my life, and I am still a Free Trader. I am not sure that I am not the most bigotted Free Trader in the House, but I am not so much a Free Trader as to shut my eyes to the terrible risks we are running at the present time . . . My suggestion . . . exclude from the country luxuries purchased from abroad.[24]

And from Labour, Arthur Henderson addressing the Trades Union Congress at Bristol on 10 September, said:

> If I am faced – and I claim to be as strong a Free Trader as any who were there – if I am faced with a large cut in the payments given to

the unemployed or a 20 per cent revenue tariff as an emergency expedient ... I am going to try the value of that experiment.[25]

Some further light can be thrown on this by looking at what was happening within the Cabinet. As early as 22 September 1931, the attention of the Cabinet was drawn to the following question to be put in Parliament by Mr Wardlaw-Milne to the President of the Board of Trade: 'Are the Government taking or do they intend to take, any steps to prevent the dumping of foreign produce into this country caused by the expectation of the imposition of Duties at an early date.'[26] The reply to be given was: '... Anyone who imports foreign [sic] goods unnecessarily is rendering a real dis-service to his country; ...and the Government are confident that both individual buyers and traders will recognise their common obligation.'[27] On 2 October the Cabinet was discussing a formula for dealing with tariffs. The Drafting Committee had produced the following: 'We ask for power to deal with and control imports, whether by prohibition, tariffs or any other measures which may be necessary.'[28] Had it not been for the considerable resistance of the Liberal ministers, who wanted to wait and see if devaluation would work to correct the balance of trade, this would undoubtedly have been accepted there and then.

The point to be made is that discussion of the tariff and its imminence was taking place as early as it did and before any suggested rise in imports. Furthermore, such were the divisions within the government on the issue that leaks to the press and the public were inevitable. For example, the morning after the Cabinet meeting that decided on introducing abnormal importations legislation an account appeared in the *Daily Telegraph* saying that the Cabinet had decided on the previous evening to introduce a bill dealing with 'dumping'.[29] Ramsey McDonald pointed this out at the next Cabinet meeting and he remarked that although the report was 'inaccurate in some important matters of detail there were passages in the paragraph which corresponded rather closely to what had occurred at the Cabinet'.[30]

A perusal of the financial and trade press of late 1931 might lead one to suspect that the tariff was an issue to be carefully considered and that nothing rushed was expected. As late as November the *Banker's Magazine* was writing, 'For whether tariffs are to be applied or whether Free Trade principles are to be adhered to...'[31] But one feels that this was a hopeful rather than a realistic position taken up by what was essentially the 'free trade' press. Immediately after the election, *The Statist* commented:

There will be a general feeling of elation or at least of relief, that the official Socialist party has been almost annihilated at the polls. . . [but] It must not be interpreted as a . . . mandate for the immediate imposition of indiscriminate protective tariffs. . .[32]

When the Abnormal Importations Act was in force a mere three weeks later, this same weekly described it as a 'dramatic move' and 'a direct outcome of what may be conveniently called "dumping" in anticipation of an import tariff'.[33] It went on to blame importers for compelling the government to take the very measures the importers most feared. Thus it may be seen that, with the likelihood of a return of a Conservative-dominated government in late 1931, and given the strong commitment of the Conservative Party to a tariff, importers were right in believing the tariff was coming and sensible in their attempt to buy before it was imposed.

I turn now to the reason given by the National Government for introducing the tariff in November 1931 and consider whether this was an excuse for protection. The questions examined are: were there 'abnormal' imports late in 1931; if so, was this because a tariff was believed to be imminent?

The general election of late October 1931 resulted in the return of the National Government – which was overwhelmingly Conservative. It was quite widely known as early as the middle of 1931 that Baldwin had a plan for an emergency tariff to be put into operation 'right away' if and when the Conservatives were returned to power.[34] There was a paper before the Cabinet in early November 1931 for the purpose of ascertaining whether or not imports were running at an excessive level.[35] The evidence was based on a comparison of Class III imports (manufactures and semi-manufactures) entering the two ports of London and Harwich in October 1930 and October 1931 (40 per cent of Class III imports were said to enter Britain through these two ports). The conclusion reached was that there was not much difference between the two months. The few days of November that were available for comparison did suggest an increase in 1931 over 1930 and on the strength of this it was suggested that the Board of Trade be empowered to impose by Order a duty of up to 100 per cent. Such alacrity to act on the basis of such slender evidence rather suggests that the Cabinet was eager to find something to substantiate its belief that protection was necessary and that legislation had to be implemented quickly.

The Abnormal Importations (Customs Duties) Bill was introduced in Parliament on 16 November 1931. The Act received Royal Assent on 20 November and came into force on 25 November (that is the date of the first Order under the Act). Second and Third Orders followed on 30 November and 19 December respectively. All three orders imposed duties of 50 per cent on a range of wholly or mainly manufactured goods. The speed of the action prompted *The Economist* to refer to the Act being 'hustled through Parliament . . .

parallelled by the promptitude with which the Board of Trade availed itself of the powers'.[36] The Act was said to be designed not to tax but to prevent goods coming in and it was further claimed that it was being introduced because of the 'abnormal' level of imports in October 1931. No one in government attempted to define 'abnormal' imports, but implicit was clearly some notion of excess. In fact the only definition of 'abnormal' seems to have come from the president of the Birmingham Chamber of Commerce, who regarded it as anything that could be made in Britain. But that can clearly be left aside as rather extreme even by Birmingham standards.

Figure 4.1 illustrates how some imports increased very sharply, while others did not, in the closing months of 1931. The data used are monthly import values.[37] The three items from Class II (largely raw materials) of the *Trade and Navigation Accounts* are the largest items in that group. Those from Class III (manufactures and semi-manufactures) range from the third largest (IIIC), iron and steel, to the second smallest (IIIE), electrical goods.

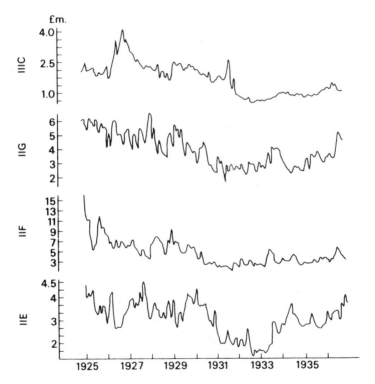

Figure 4.1   Deseasonalised Monthly Imports, Values of Selected Items, 1925–36

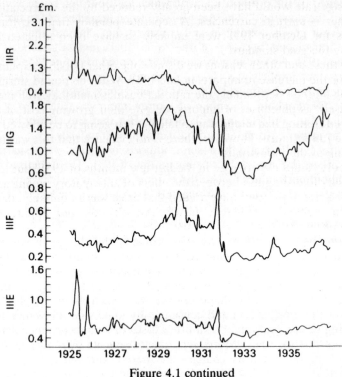

Figure 4.1 continued

The point should be made that a change in values could come from either price or volume changes. Prices in trade were falling throughout the depression, but when Britain left the gold standard in September 1931 she allowed sterling to depreciate for some months until it was around 30 per cent lower in relation to the gold currencies. The exchange rate was stabilised in early 1932 and manipulated via the Exchange Equalisation Account. British trade should therefore have been given assistance by a depreciating currency at roughly the same time as the tariff was imposed. The difficulty is to separate the price effects of the tariff from the effects of the falling exchange rate. Of course many countries either immediately realigned their currencies with sterling, or their abandonment of gold during 1929–31 left their currency in a close relationship to sterling. In other words, in many cases there was little price effect arising from the exchange rate and little significant exclusion of many imports into the UK;[38] the bulk of British trade was with countries whose currencies moved with hers (though that part of trade was largely raw materials and food) and the upward pressure on prices resulting from depreciation of the exchange rate would have been greatly reduced by the depreciation of other countries' currencies. A separate point is that the trade figures for October 1931 were unlikely to have been affected by leaving the gold standard.

For these and other reasons we dismiss one other possible explanation for the increase in imports in late 1931. With the pound sterling sinking after 21 September, the rational businessman may well have increased his purchases of imports, despite their growing cost, if he believed sterling had a long way to fall and was going to be allowed to fall the full distance. However, there is no evidence that this was the thinking of the industrialist.

Import values clearly rose in the last few months of 1931, but it is necessary to distinguish between the effect of anticipatory buying and that of a rise in prices. I have argued that price was an unlikely, or at most a feeble, contributory factor. An obvious and apparently uncomplicated way of resolving the price question would be to look at quantities on their own, for it is primarily the change in volume that concerns us. Unfortunately, this is not as simple as it at first appears. The quantities of many manufactured goods were not recorded in the *Trade and Navigation Accounts*. For others, quantity is recorded in a wholly inappropriate way (such as by weight for sophisticated machinery) and consequently makes no allowance for changing design and quality. In other cases dissimilar products have been lumped together. Moreover, quantity on its own may ignore some of the relative price changes that were taking place, for, while prices in general were falling, they were not all falling at the same rate and purchases would have been made on the basis of individual price movements.

In spite of some of these difficulties, it was possible to investigate some quantity movements for eight sub-groups of that important group of manufactures, iron and steel. Figure 4.2 presents the graph of four of these items within iron and steel. The figures plotted are the deseasonalised monthly quantity figures, and it is clear from the graph that in all four cases (and they are typical of all the groups within this classification) quantities imported in the closing months of 1931 were rising, in spite of the rapidly depreciating currency and in the face of the collapse of world trade. This seems to support strongly our suspicion that considerable pre-ordering was going on.

A further possible means of examining the problem is to compare the experience of goods on which a tariff was expected and imposed with the experience of those without a tariff. Broadly speaking, the tariff was anticipated and fell on manufactured goods – Class III of the *Trade and Navigation Accounts*. Class I (food, etc.) was exempt, as was the great bulk of Class II (raw materials). To support our case, when we compare items in Class III with those of Classes I and II we

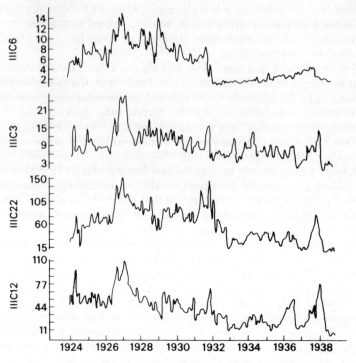

Figure 4.2   Deseasonalised Monthly Imports, Quantities of Iron, 1924–38

should find the latter two unexceptional while the former should
show a rise. Such a comparison is acceptable in that on theoretical
grounds we would expect Class I and Class II imports to have been
less price-elastic than those of Class III, and empirical studies bear
this out. The available estimates of price elasticities of demand for
the type of disaggregated British imports that are our concern range
from −0.99 to −0.67 for Class I as a whole through an even lower
level of −0.32 and −0.40 for raw cotton and wood and timber
respectively, to the much more price-elastic manufactured items of
Class III.[39] For pottery and glassware the estimate is −5.9; close
behind is cotton manufactures at −4.7.[40] Some of the others are
much lower but, nevertheless, all items are in excess of unity. Therefore, sterling depreciation producing a uniform upward pressure on
prices should, *ceteris paribus*, have manifested itself the more clearly
in price-inelastic goods. With quantity relatively steady and prices
rising, values could have been expected to rise more steeply for Class
I and Class II imports. But in fact, when we examine the monthly
import figures for these items and, indeed, all other items, we find

rather that the values of Class III imports rose more than the others. This suggests that the comparison between the items is valid. We can conclude that the rising values owed more to pre-tariff ordering than to the price pressure from a depreciating pound.

Some measure of support for this notion of anticipatory ordering can be found in the figures for a few years earlier. In the budget of April 1925, Britain returned to the gold standard at a revalued rate. The return was widely anticipated, as was a return to protection for certain 'key' industries, most notably cutlery, vehicles and silk goods. When we look at the import figures for vehicles and cutlery (Figure 4.1, III E and III R) we find that there is a great surge in imports in the two months preceding the budget announcement and a clear lack of it in all the other commodities. The pre-ordering here is interesting and it does suggest an awareness on the part of businessmen and a certain leaking of information about the tariff, both sufficient to produce a rather dramatic rise in the imports concerned, and this at a time when revaluation was going to exert a downward pressure on prices.[41] It seems reasonable to conclude that exactly the same process was operating in 1931 and we can imterpret the jumps in 1931 in this light.

Having established that the conditions for this perfectly rational action and its practice were present, it remains to suggest its extent. One measure that should indicate how much was being bought in anticipation is the percentage deviation of the deseasonalised figure from the trend figure (see Appendix for details on how the series of

Table 4.1 *Percentage Deviations from the Trend of the Deseasonalised Values of Monthly Imports*

	October 1931	November 1931
Class II		
Wood & timber	−12.56	− 2.05
Raw cotton	−34.44	+ 7.57
Raw wool	+ 5.89	+14.23
Class III		
Iron & steel manufactures	+17.23	+71.16
Cutlery & hardware	+59.47	+105.55
Electrical goods	+19.74	+88.77
Machinery	+34.57	+39.34
Vehicles	+41.94	− 4.90
Class II total	−14.70	0.33
Class III total	25.47	44.55

Table 4.2   *Percentage Deviations from the Trend of the Deseasonalised Quantities of Monthly Imports of Iron and Steel Manufactures*

	October 1931	November 1931
Steel girders, beams, joists & pillars	16.37	79.73
Tubes	13.14	64.31
Steel blooms, billets, slabs	31.12	73.79
Steel bars, rods, angles, shapes & sections	−7.37	57.16

British imports were deseasonalised). With seasonality removed from the monthly figures, the deviation from the trend provides a value that can arise only from a random disturbance. Table 4.1 gives these percentage values for eight commodities taken from Classes II and III of the *Trade and Navigation Accounts*. Of the three most important items of raw material imports, raw cotton was actually quite substantially below the trend value for October and wood and timber was also below; raw wool was slightly above. In November, wood and timber was again below trend and the other two a little above. For items in Class III, on the other hand, the positive deviation from the trend was quite remarkable. In nearly half the cases, imports were more than 50 per cent higher than expected. The most dramatic increase was that of cutlery and hardware in November 1931. The point is strengthened when Class II and III totals are taken. Class II is below trend for the total of the two months, while Class III as a whole is 35 per cent above. The quantity figures for iron and steel manufactures (Table 4.2) show the great increase in volume of these imports over the expected figure.

To sum up, there were indeed some abnormally high imports in the closing months of 1931, but they appear to have been brought about by the business community's belief that a tariff was imminent and their attempt to buy before duties were introduced.

This chapter then has argued that protection was not simply a response to economic depression. It is unlikely that dumping was significant in the period preceding the introduction of the general tariff, although allegations of dumping may have been responsible for intensifying the protectionist mood. It seems that claims of abnormal imports in late 1931 were exaggerated, and that the increases that did occur were caused by anticipation of import duties, since the principle of protection was already accepted by most Conservatives in the early 1930s and a detailed scheme had been drawn up by late 1930, ready to be introduced as soon as the Conservatives returned to power.

Notes

1   There are many examples but typical of the textbook version is Derek H. Aldcroft, *The Inter-War Economy: Britain 1919 – 1939* (1970), p. 285.
2   There is an early hint that it was not entirely due to the crisis in F. C. C. Benham, *Great Britain Under Protection* (1941), p. 21.
3   In Hugh J. Schonfield (ed.), *The Book of British Industries* (1933), p. 205.
4   W. M. Corden, *Trade Policy and Economic Welfare* (1974); Jacob Viner, *Dumping: A Problem in International Trade* (1923); Gottfried von Haberler, *The Theory of International Trade* (1936).
5   Haberler, op. cit., p. 315.
6   Gerald D. Feldman, *Iron and Steel in the German Inflation 1916–1923* (1977).
7   Haberler, op. cit., p. 315.
8   The Safeguarding of Industries Act, Part II, Section 3, covered dumping and allowed for a duty of 33⅓ per cent, *ad valorem*. The onus of proof lay on those making the claims. The definition used was that of differential selling prices after allowance had been made for transport costs and selling charges.
9   Viner (op. cit, p. 2) shows that the experience of the US Tariff Commission was similar. Of 146 complaints of dumping received, all but 23 were severe competition. The 23 were alleged cases of price discrimination.
10 Public Record Office, CAB 58/130. CR62, Iron and Steel Committee, Forgings and Coatings Section.
11 Public Record Office, CAB 58/128. CR25, Iron and Steel Committee.
12 Public Record Office, CAB 24/224, CP 275. II, Alleged instances of dumping.
13 Ian McLeod, *Neville Chamberlain* (1961), p. 154.
14 John Ramsden, *The Age of Balfour and Baldwin 1902–1940* (1978), p. 321.
15 Particularly by the one-man campaign launched in 1926 by Clive Morrison-Bell. His physical model of tariff walls gained enormous publicity all over Europe and America and resulted in a book, *Tariff Walls: a European Crusade* (1930).
16 *Beveridge Papers, Tariffs*, Vol. I, Letter, 11 July 1930.
17 ibid., Letter, 31 October 1930.
18 Quoted by Samuel H. Beer, *Modern British Politics* (1969), p. 288.
19 L. S. Amery, *My Political Life*, vol. III (1955), p. 22.
20 Beer, op. cit., p. 289.
21 Amery, op. cit., pp. 21, 22.
22 *The Times*, 21 May 1931, p. 9, col. 1.
23 Sir John Simon, *Parliamentary Debates*, 15 September 1931, Vol. 256, Col. 729.
24 *Parliamentary Debates*, 1930–1, Vol. 256, Col. 331 and Col. 729.
25 *The Times*, 11 September 1931, p. 7, col. 3.
26 Public Record Office, CAB 23/68.
27 ibid.
28 ibid., p. 334.
29 *Daily Telegraph*, 3 October 1931.
30 Public Record Office, CAB 23/69, 13 November 1931.
31 *Bankers' Magazine*, November 1931, p. 650.
32 *The Statist*, 31 October 1931, p. 583.
33 21 November 1931, p. 817.
34 See, for example, *The Economist*, 25 July 1931, p. 165.
35 Public Record Office, CAB 24/224, CP 274.
36 *The Economist*, 28 November 1931, p. 993.
37 The data are given in *Accounts Relating to the Trade and Navigation of the United Kingdom* (monthly) 1925–36. The data have been deseasonalised, where necessary, using the CSO mixed model.

38   The depreciation of sterling was followed almost immediately by Canada, India,
     Iceland, Denmark, Egypt, Norway and Sweden. This meant that between 1929
     and 1932 the total number of countries that had depreciated in relation to gold was
     32.
39   M. Fg. Scott, *A Study of United Kingdom Imports* (1963).
40   T. C. Chang, *Cyclical Movements in the Balance of Payments* (1951).
41   *The Economist*, 18 July 1925, p. 99, recognised that the forestalling of duties was
     one of the reasons for the increased figures in these months.

5

The Growth of Protectionist Pressure

Baldwin has a policy, a little fiscal policy,
Based upon suggestions by his followers and friends,
(Noted very carefully and treasured up with reverence)
Little bits of tariffs and of quotas and of preference,
Safeguarding and subsidies and other odds and ends.

Baldwin gets a telegram, a little daily telegram,
(From Amery or Chamberlain or Brentford, let us say)
Or a letter, or a phone-call, or a postcard, just a penny one,
(From Beaverbrook or Rothermere or practically anyone),
To tell him what his policy had better be today.

Baldwin keeps a diary, a little pocket diary,
For noting down his policy at each successive stage,
He knows what it was yesterday because he made a note for it;
But neither he nor we can tell (although he'd have us vote for it)
His policy tomorrow, when he's turned another page.

[MacFlecknoe Verses]

Links with Nineteenth-Century Protectionist Movements

From around the middle of the nineteenth century until the First
World War, Great Britain pursued, and advocated abroad, a policy
of free trade. A typical activity was a delegation from the Leeds
Chamber of Commerce to Vienna in 1865 'to educate the Austrians
in our principles of Free Trade'.[1] A small number of minor duties
remained on some items throughout the century, but they were not
protective in design or practice. The guiding principle in Britain's
international trading relations throughout this period was freedom in
the home market for world goods, and securing 'most-favoured-
nation' treatment abroad. Of course the policy was never universally

popular and, after a brief spell in the middle of the nineteenth century when it seemed the developing international economy would adopt it widely, it faltered and the growth of protective devices multiplied around the trading world after 1870, and from then on up to the First World War.

In Britain, too, there were always those who were opposed to free trade. The Fiscal Reform League had been formed in 1870 for the purpose of lobbying for the adoption of moderate duties on foreign manufactures. There was much discussion and much support from some chambers of commerce.[2] As soon as an industry felt the pinch of international competition there would follow demands for protection of the domestic market. The National Fair Trade League was formed in 1881 by just some such suffering manufactures. The tariff reform movement that grew up in these years worked diligently on all sides and was closely associated with the movements for protection and imperial preference both at home and in Empire countries. Some preference was being extended to Britain by Empire countries by the end of the century, and these countries were seeking something in return from Britain. Joseph Chamberlain gave the tariff reformers fresh encouragement in the 1890s when he became Colonial Secretary and made clear where his sympathies lay. He later led the tariff reform movement. However, none of these activities bore any fruit. The 1906 elections were contested with the issues of protection and imperial preference very clearly in the forefront, but the electorate was not persuaded. So at the outbreak of the First World War Britain remained firmly attached to the free trade doctrine, having come through years of increasing international competition and some industrial recession without really wavering on the policy.

There were of course many politicians, businessmen and others involved in the tariff reform movement in the early twentieth century who were again active in the war years and in the 1920s, and a dominating theme in the protectionist case continued to be the role of Empire and imperial preference. (At its inaugural meeting in July 1903, the Tariff Reform League declared itself 'for the defence and development of the industrial interests of the British Empire'.[3]) Many of those associated with the movement never left the protectionist case. L. S. Amery was a founding member of the executive committee and Bonar Law carried the protectionist banner from before until after the war. W. A. S. Hewins, professor of economics at the London School of Economics, was secretary to the Tariff Commission in 1903, and was said to write anonymously for the Tariff Reform League. He was responsible for Joseph Chamberlain's decision to undertake the tariff reform campaign.[4] Hewins was again prominent in the work of the Empire Industries Association from 1924 onwards, as we shall see later. Percy Ashley, another 'imperialist' from the London School of

Economics, was adviser to Balfour – the important tariff reformer – and became secretary to the very powerful Import Duties Advisory Committee of 1932–9. And so on.

Such threads of continuity do not necessarily mean, however, that firm origins of the 1930s protection can be traced to 1903 or the years around it. Benjamin Brown claimed '. . . it is only a hop, a skip and a jump from these early tariff reformers to the Ottawa Conference of 1932. . .',[5] and there were emotional scenes in the Commons when Neville Chamberlain introduced the tariff legislation of 1932 and claimed to be fulfilling the dreams of his father Joseph, but a more accurate perception was that of McGuire:

> It is said that the country turned over from free trade to protection with the imposition of the general tariff under the Import Duties Act of 1932; but it is more correct to state that this Act was the culmination of a movement which had been gathering force ever since its supporters had received a serious setback at the elections of 1923.[6]

I would revise that date back to the First World War. War and depression have proved to be two common sources of protection and it was the First World War that proved the catalyst for Britain. Some protective duties were introduced then, but more importantly a great clamouring for protection developed, with the various claimants pointing to the pivotal nature of their industry and their respective contributions to national security.

The Balfour of Burleigh Committee of 1918, whose brief was to consider commercial and industrial policy after the war, was strong in its advocacy of a tariff, particularly for 'pivotal' industries. It recommended that 'the imposition of a wide range of tariff duties . . . should come into force immediately on the conclusion of war'.[7] The industries described as 'key' or pivotal were to be kept alive 'either by loans, by subsidy, by tariff . . . or in the last event by government manufacture'.[8] Other industries of 'real importance' were to qualify if it were clear that they were in danger of being weakened by foreign competition.

It was in this atmosphere that large parts of British industry were converted to protection and it is here that the sources of the interwar protectionist movement can be found. An outstanding example of this, already touched on in the discussion of dumping in Chapter 4, was the iron and steel industry.

The Iron and Steel Industry's Search for Protection

The iron and steel industry would always attract attention in an investigation such as this both by virtue of its size and because of its importance as a supplier to other industries. It is perhaps ironic that in 1932 it was the only industry in Britain where the final product was eventually taxed at a lower rate than the inputs (probably the first time in British tariff history that this had happened) and the difference was of sufficient magnitude to produce a very low effective rate of protection for the industry as a whole.[9]

The iron and steel industry gained early encouragement for a protective tariff from the strong feelings expressed during the First World War about the need to safeguard vital industries. The Board of Trade committee set up in 1916 to consider the position of the iron, steel and engineering trades after the war was initially under the chairmanship of Sir Clarendon Hyde, a well-known free trader in the industry; Sir Hugh Bell was also a prominent member. Clarendon Hyde's chairmanship was unacceptable to the industry for, on matters of protection, 'it is not too much to say that his views are diametrically opposed to those of the vast majority of his fellow manufacturers'.[10] Lobbying by the industry for his removal was successful and the Board of Trade finally replaced Hyde with Scoby-Smith – equally well-known as a protectionist. Not too surprisingly, the Committee's report of June 1918 was strongly in favour of protection.[11]

The evidence presented to this Committee insisted 'almost unanimously that competition through dumping ... had reached such a pitch that the production of iron and steel in Great Britain was seriously restricted and imperilled'.[12] The committee was convinced that for 'the future safeguarding of the iron and steel industries it will be necessary to establish a system of protective duties'.[13] The committee went on to make several recommendations. Besides encouraging combinations, it suggested that anti-dumping legislation be introduced, that all imports should show their mark or origin and 'that customs duties be imposed upon all imported iron and steel and manufactures thereof...'.[14]

The iron and steel industry recognised the need to organise, amongst other things, to campaign for protection. On Armistice Day 1918 the National Federation of Iron and Steel manufacturers (NFISM) was formed 'in recognition by the industry and the government' that the industry's problems required a stronger central organisation.[15] The Federation was made up of the directors of leading companies.

War or the fear of war dominated the debate on protection over the next few years and imperial preference was almost always an integral part of the protectionist case.[16] But it became clear in the three years of coalition government following the war that the electorate was far from persuaded to protection. In a fourteen-month spell, seven by-elections were decided on this issue. In late 1919 an attempt was made at legislation to cope with three different aspects of trading competition: dumping; countries whose over-depreciated currencies gave them unfair advantage in the British market; and key industries. But the opposition to such legislation was strong and the Bill was withdrawn.

The passing of the Safeguarding of Industries Act in 1921 was something of a victory for a small section of protectionist industrialists and Conservative MPs, although the value of goods affected (in spite of the fact that 6,500 items were listed) was very low. The passing of the Act probably owes more to the comparative insignificance of the items covered and to the emphasis placed on the pivotal nature of the industries – in spite of Wedgwood Benn's comments.[17]

The fact that the electorate was no nearer persuasion on the issue of a tariff was demonstrated in the 1923 general election. There is a line of argument in political theory that runs: a government will act to maximise its chances of re-election and will therefore present to the consumer what it believes to be the most acceptable bundle of policies. This has a certain superficial application to 1923. If, as seems reasonable given the lack of factor mobility in the 1920s, we reject the notion that the benefits to factors of production tend to be dispersed by competition through the whole of the economy, producers would be the gainers under protection.

In 1923 the Conservatives were seeking re-election and presented their bundle of policies to the electorate. But one policy stood out above all others and the election of that year can be said to have been contested very largely on the issue of protection. The government appears to have had the backing of some of British industry, which at this time was becoming much more interested in tariffs. For example, part of the textile trade had sought an Order under the Safeguarding Act a matter of weeks before the election, and the iron and steel industry was working diligently for a tariff. The motor car industry actively supported the protectionist case and did everything it could to persuade its workers to vote Conservative. The National Union of Manufacturers campaigned vigorously to win over the working classes.[18] Yet the electorate rejected the package firmly. It is tempting to see in this behaviour a sophisticated electorate at work accurately perceiving its prospective gains and losses, for it seems to have been the case that the electorate feared the prospect of dearer food that would result from a tariff. Foodstuffs and raw materials were the principal exports of the Empire to the British market and in order to extend to the Empire the preferences they expected and were beginning to demand by way of reciprocation, tariffs or other restrictive devices would have had to have been placed on imports of foreign food and raw materials. This was welcomed by neither producers nor consumers. It is still not clear why the protectionist faction did not

make greater progress with this problem, though it has to be said it
was not an easy one.

The iron and steel industry was the only major industry that persistently continued to seek protection throughout the 1920s. In June
1925 an application was made to the president of the Board of Trade
for duties (under the Safeguarding Act) on pig iron, wrought iron,
heavy steel products and wire. On rejecting the application at the end
of the year, Prime Minister Baldwin said that safeguarding a basic
industry of this magnitude would have repercussions that might have
been held to have been in conflict with the government's declaration
in regard to a general tariff.[19] Most of the NFISM's executive committee and the director, Sir William Larke, were enthusiastic tariff
reformers, and in early 1926 they gave their support to a sub-section
of the industry, wire, when it made an independent application. But
this application was rejected on the same grounds. The main application was renewed in 1927, but again it was turned down by reference
to the original decision.

The Iron and Steel Confederation tried a slightly different
approach the following year (1928) by asking the government to set
up a committee to investigate competition in the home market. This
was refused by Baldwin, although he did say that if the Conservatives
were returned at the general election of 1929 the iron and steel
industry could make out a case under the safeguarding provisions.
This was a shift from the government's earlier position and, together
with the increasing openness of the Conservatives over protection,
led the industry to be hopeful for the immediate future. After the
election of 1929, when Labour formed the government, the position
was further considered and an inquiry set up as a sub-committee of
the Committee of Civil Research.[20] It may seem ironical that, in spite
of the fact that a free trade Labour government was now in power,
whose official policy was to abolish even existing duties, the real
hopes of the iron and steel industry built up, but it should be borne in
mind that there were Labour members who had shown sympathy
with safeguarding Orders when applied to manufactures of their
respective constituencies.

Perhaps the key to the lack of success of the iron and steel industry's search for protection in the mid 1920s, apart from the nervous-
ness of a Conservative government over introducing a tariff on a
major industry when the defeat of 1923 was still fresh in their minds,
lies in the fact that, in the first place, the iron and steel industry was a
supplier of inputs to much of British industry. Although the iron and
steel industry argued that protection would allow them full capacity
utilisation and economies of scale such as to produce lower prices,
much of British industry remained understandably sceptical of this
argument, and feared that the price of their inputs would in fact rise.

(The Shipbuilding Employers' Federation was particularly anxious over this. Shipbuilding was the biggest single user of iron and steel and we can see from the effective rate of protection how their fears were justified.[21]) In the second place, there was a division within the iron and steel industry itself. The production of pig iron, its conversion into steel ingots and the rolling of ingots into blooms, billets, slabs and other semi-finished products constituted the larger 'heavy' section of the industry. The re-rolling of 'semis' into various shapes and sizes was the much smaller section, sometimes referred to as the 'light' part of the industry. But re-rolling was also carried out by the 'heavy' part; indeed, it was estimated that 50 per cent of re-rolling was carried out by steelmakers rather than simple re-rollers.[22] During the 1920s British imports of iron and steel were principally 'semis' from the continent. Not surprisingly, the re-rolling and finishing section was loud in its opposition to a tariff on its raw materials. The defence of tariffs by the 'heavy' part was expressed in the evidence given to the Committee on Iron and Steel Industries by Walmsley (director of Messrs Blockow, Vaughan and Co. Ltd):

It is by no means certain that if we had safeguarding . . . the re-roller would have to pay remarkably more for their British supply of semi-finished material than they do from the continent. We hope and most of us believe, that we could by increasing production so reduce our costs that we should come very much nearer to the continental price. . .[23]

In fact, as Mr Scarf explained in his evidence to the Committee,[24] the British Steel Re-Rollers Association was formed in May 1924 in order to combat the steelmakers' attempt to obtain duties on imports of semi-products. Indeed, the evidence of the steel sheet industry was that they led the world in galvanised sheet exports (with exports far in excess of all other producers put together) because they could get cheap supplies of continental Basic Bessemer steel sheets, bars and slabs.

The antagonism between the two parts of the industry was deep. In his evidence, Walmsley went on to remark,

with all respect to the re-rollers I would suggest that in all these questions of safeguarding they have figured too largely . . . perhaps it would be going too far if I described him [re-roller] as a parasite.... [but] if some went out of business because of safeguarding, the work he is doing now would be done by the Steelmaker.[25]

As mentioned above, strong opposition to a tariff on iron and steel came from other industries too. Sir John Lithgow of the Shipbuilding

Employers' Federation stated that his industry was opposed to the safeguarding of iron and steel. A note of bitterness crept into his evidence when he pointed out that there had been 'times when the interests of British steelmakers had led them to supply foreign ship-builders . . . at a lower price than the home shipbuilders'.[26] Of course, the great bulk of evidence heard by the Committee came from within the iron and steel industry, and as the 'heavy' part was so dominant the great majority of witnesses favoured protection.

The iron and steel industry, and particularly the heavy part, was to exert constant pressure on government. Yet the 'key' nature of the industry presented a dilemma: while it was in one way sensible to safeguard such an industry against destruction by even legitimate foreign competition (given the uncertainty of the international economy), at the same time this meant increasing prices for much of British industry. When it is remembered that the raising of prices (associated with improving confidence) had become an aim of policy by 1930/1, the timing of the introduction of a tariff is perhaps more readily understood.

In summary, the potential benefits to producers from protection would not have been dispersed by competition throughout the economy because of comparative factor immobility, and we should not be surprised to find industry increasingly exerting pressure for a tariff. Further, it was widely accepted that from the First World War the iron and steel industry was suffering from slow technical change and from being made up of scattered small units unable to exploit economies of scale. The obstacle to the iron and steel industry's success was its central role as supplier of a major input to much of the rest of the industrial sector. The industry nevertheless kept the subject in the news. Some of the significance of the industry's fight lies in the fact that it had clearly alerted the rest of British industry in the 1920s to protective possibilities, and in and out of Parliament had helped to foster the protectionist mood.

Business Pressure

The story of the origins of the 1932 tariff can be told in a number of ways. Even supposing agreement on the inappropriateness of the policy-of-crisis explanation, as argued in the previous chapter, the story of the medium-term origins can still take a variety of forms. It might be presented in terms of high politics, as some would have it,[27] where a relatively small group with power manipulated others and achieved their own political goals. In this case, Neville Chamberlain the pragmatic protectionist, Austen Chamberlain his less clear-thinking but emotionally more committed half-brother, together with

Amery, Page Croft and others, out-manoeuvred their opposition, be it Labour, Liberal or Conservative. Still in political terms, it might be seen as the product of the work of interested constituency groups,[28] in this case the protectionist West Midlands (the home of Amery, Chamberlain, Hannon, and others). It might even be argued, as is hinted above, that the tariff reformers of pre-1914 vintage were still strong in 1922 and that the Conservative Party was effectively protectionist at that stage. This line of argument would say there was no need for new converts, and no need for lobbying, for they simply had to wait for the right moment to implement policies already prepared. The failure of 1923 and Baldwin's pledge of 1924 postponed that moment, but the time would come again.

Some of these views have some appeal and some a certain amount of truth, but all of these accounts neglect the area of the economic origins of pressure. After all, the story of the coming of tariffs in other countries is frequently told almost exclusively in terms of business interest pressure groups,[29] and it should be no surprise to find interested parties behaving in a similar fashion in Britain in the twentieth century. Indeed it is surprising to find that in the 1950s a book on British politics appeared that talked of the 'spreading "grey zone" of business influence in Parliament'. There is no reason now, and there should not have been one then, to suppose that this was something new in the 1950s.[30]

There are good economic grounds for expecting the emergence and growth of protectionism in Britain in the 1920s. Protection has frequently been born in war and in times of economic recession. The First World War was particularly damaging to Britain's trade, and throughout the 1920s, although by some measures of economic growth the economy performed moderately well, by other indicators, such as unemployment and the loss of potential output, the economy was suffering more than most.

Another important pressure for protection arises out of desire to solve a balance of payments problem. The pressure to protect presupposes that imbalances between strong and weak countries are not corrected by movements of labour, capital or technology. The changed international conditions of the years after the First World War certainly inhibited the flow of resources that had characterised the period before 1914, and so produced conditions in which this pressure could prosper. More than this, where the imbalance cannot be corrected by exchange rate adjustments, the pressure for protection is likely to be intensified. Given the concern with the exchange rate established in 1925, and the considerable commitment to that fixed rate under the new gold standard, such a pressure was greatly increased. Of course after September 1931 the adverse trade balance may have been redressed by means of the depreciating exchange rate,

70 DEPRESSION AND PROTECTIONISM

and this was when Keynes withdrew his advocacy of a tariff, but diehards like Amery continued to push the tariff, believing that 'a comprehensive tariff' was the only way to restrict imports.[31]

Table 5.1 presents the basic information from the British balance of payments for the 1920s as available at the time. Of course the figures were not presented then as they are now, but the table brings together the information published by the Board of Trade, which is in essence the current account of the balance of payments. The table shows that, to contemporary eyes, the trade balance, which is what they were most concerned with, was deteriorating quite badly in the first half of the 1920s, although it did level off in the second half of the decade. This was more or less reflected in the balance on current account, though there was more improvement in the latter before the dramatic collapse of 1931. None of this is evidence of pressure, simply the backdrop, but it does suggest that conditions were 'right' and of course reflects the difficulties British industrialists were facing at home and abroad.

The line of argument that requires development is that over these years (say 1919–31) the political life of the country was increasingly influenced by businessmen, although there were undoubtedly conflicting pressures at work, from Bonar Law the ironmaker, through Baldwin the steelmaker and the Chamberlains the screw manufacturers. According to one account, between 1919 and 1939 on average one-third of the Conservative Party in the Commons were employers or managers.[32] And while it would be dangerous to draw conclusions

Table 5.1   *Contemporary Current Account Estimates 1920–31 (£m.)*

	Visible trade balance[1]		Balance of invisibles		Balance on current account[1]	
1920	−385		595		210	
1922	−180	−181[2]	325	325[2]	145	144[2]
1923	−216	−208	300	348	84	140
1924	−355	−338	370	410	15	72
1925	−396	−392	414	438	18	46
1926	−466	−464	465	449	−1	−15
1927	−389	−387	488	469	99	82
1928	−352	−351	508	475	156	123
1929	−381	−381	517	484	136	103
1930	−387	−386	431	414	44	28
1931	−411	−408	301	304	−110	−104

[1] excludes gold.
[2] revised figures produced in the period.
Sources: 1920 and 1922: *Board of Trade Journal*, March 1923; 1923 onwards: *Statistical Abstract for the United Kingdom.*

too rapidly from a simple count of heads, bearing in mind the diversity of motives that take people into Parliament and conscious too that numbers alone do not accurately reflect the strength of respective groupings, clearly the larger the numbers were, the greater was the chance that business interests were represented and the higher the probability that business demands would be heard, that numbers could be found for support and so on. We know that industrialists were alert to the opportunities for potential gains from protection. Arthur Chamberlain (chairman of Messrs Tubes Ltd and director of several other companies) put the case both succinctly and powerfully when he warned at an earlier date:

> Give us protection, and we manufacturers will show you something in the way of rings and trusts and syndicates that you little dream of ... I could make more money in any evening in the House of Commons by arranging for the taxation of my opponent's necessities and for the maintenance of a free market for myself than I could make by honest industry in a month.[33]

Business groups were accustomed to organising themselves for specific objectives in the nineteenth century and of course had a focus in the chambers of commerce. From late in the nineteenth century, an increasing number of manufacturers began to support the Conservative Party with the avowed intention of securing tariffs.

Several business organisations had been formed in the First World War with a view to defending business interests. Many of them were direct descendants of the prewar tariff movements, but others were the product of new concerns raised by war. In January 1915, soon after the outbreak of war, a Unionist Business Committee was formed in the House of Commons to protect the interest of business in time of war. This Committee made suggestions based on the 'expert assistance of the Tariff Commission'.[34] *The Economist* was moved to remark: 'the obvious truth is that many of our wealthy manufactures are using their power, funds and influence to secure the imposition of tariffs.'[35] A high point of business pressure for protection came with the publication of a tariff scheme adopted by the London Chamber of Commerce on 25 May 1916.

The Federation of British Industries (FBI) was formed in 1916 and it worked diligently to present the views of industry to government. It was protective in outlook. In 1916 the British Commonwealth Union was established 'to form a solid business group in Parliament'. A fundamental element of the BCU's programme was tariff reform: 'It was to press for the protective tariffs and restriction of imports discussed at the Paris Economic Conference of 1916 and in the Balfour of Burleigh report on post War commercial policy.'[36] Turner shows how the BCU attracted a considerable membership and while it failed in its objectives of monopolising communications between business and government and in imposing itself on the Conservative Party machine, this was due not to the weakness of business interest but to the strength and diversity of that interest.

In the grave recession of 1921 the Conservatives exploited the collapse in trade for their protectionist ends. A powerful deputation from the National Union of Manufacturers (NUM) visited Baldwin, the president of the Board of Trade, urging prompt action. Baldwin agreed.[37] The Safeguarding of Industries Bill soon followed, being introduced on 2 June 1921. It had no difficulty in its passage through Parliament and became law on 1 October. It was a clear case of protection (even if only of modest extent) resulting from business pressure. The NUM continued to keep the pressure up, with the result that the greater part of British industry was encouraged to lend support to the campaign of 1923. According to Taylor, the 1923 election was 'the only election in British history fought solely and specifically on Protection'.[38] Baldwin was now the leader of the party and has been accused of behaving like most manufacturers of steel and thinking only of the home market.[39] The Chairman of the Conservative Party in the late 1920s agreed: 'Protection had been in Baldwin's mind ever since his business days.'[40]

A key figure in the British Commonwealth Union was Patrick Hannon, a former vice-president of the Tariff Reform League, and later secretary of the Industrial Group in the House of Commons (1921–9) and a vice-president of the FBI. Hannon and several others of the BCU were to carry on their activities under a new banner over the next few years, that of the Empire Industries Association. Hannon even played a part in founding the Association in 1924 for the purpose of lobbying for a tariff. This Association had tremendous support from backbenchers, who showed increasing intransigence from 1924 onwards, resenting the decision to drop tariffs that year but comforting themselves with the assurance that no Conservative government would keep such a pledge.[41] If for no other reason, the Association is important in that it has been given much of the credit for the coming of the tariff. For example, Amery remarked of it that it was destined to 'exercise a decisive influence in Parliament when Free Trade was finally swept away ...'.[42] On the introduction of the tariff in 1932, he commented that 'most of the spadework in Parliament and in the country had in any case been done by my colleagues of the Empire Industries Association ...'.[43] It is worth looking at the work of this particular organisation as an example of how some interests worked to secure their objectives.

The first meeting of the executive committee of the Empire Industries Association was held in April 1924 in the offices of the British

Commonwealth Union. Those present included members of the BCU and members of the Industrial Group in the House of Commons.[44] The hard core from which the executive committee over the next few years was taken was also to be found at this meeting: Hewins, Terrell, Hannon, Williams, Solomon. The interesting absentees at the meeting were Amery, Page Croft and Neville Chamberlain, since Hannon claimed that he and these three formed this Association.[45] Chamberlain, presumably because of his position in the Cabinet, never attended, and there is no evidence of his participation apart from speaking at public meetings that had been organised by the EIA. Amery, who appeared at the second meeting, had undoubtedly done much of the preparatory work in 1924 and he became prominent later. Page Croft made his first appearance at the third meeting on 2 July 1925; within a year he was chairman, a position he held for some years. Sir Robert Horne was invited to be chairman but while expressing himself flattered at the invitation he excused himself on the grounds that his business interests were too pressing. However, the real reason emerged at a later meeting when a letter from Horne was read out stating that because of the free trade sympathies of his constituency he was unable to play any part in the organisation.[46]

The objectives of the Association were stated to be the cultivation of British public opinion on the importance of Empire markets and the extension of empire preference and of the safeguarding of home industries in view of the extent to which the latter were suffering at the hands of foreigners. Hannon advocated taking up work immediately in favour of protection and imperial preference. It is also of interest to note that as early as this first meeting the steel industry was involved, it being reported that the industry had been sounded out and was prepared to give financial support to the Association immediately. Hannon urged the members at the second meeting of the need to act quickly in view of the position of steel.[47]

The first general meeting of the Association did not take place until February 1926 and was not followed by another until August of that year. At this second meeting, a resolution was passed urging 'an extensive system of Imperial Preference ... Great Britain must impose tariffs on foreign imports'.[48] It was further stated that ' ... everyone who has previously striven for the same cause as Protectionists and Tariff Reformers are [sic] welcome into the Empire Industries Association'.[49] The council submitted proposals to the Chancellor for the budget, and pressed the president of the Board of Trade to receive deputations from industries seeking import duties. There can thus be no doubt about the Association's protectionist position. In fact very little else was ever discussed at meetings, be they council, general, parliamentary or executive meetings. Further, the EIA had accurately perceived one crucial aspect of the problem, namely that posed by the iron and steel industry. If a tariff were imposed on iron and steel then, as Baldwin had remarked, in view of its importance to the rest of industry a general tariff could not be far behind; and it appears that working with this simple guiding principle the EIA persistently supported the cause of iron and steel.

The EIA became a most powerful pressure group in the course of the next few years, cultivating the press and public opinion assiduously. Rothermere and Beaverbrook had already shown sympathy, although Beaverbrook differed on one fundamental point, as he wrote to Amery in 1928: 'I am opposed to a special tariff on Iron and Steel . . . I deplore what appears to me to be an attempt by Baldwin to make the best of both fiscal worlds. . .'[50] The Association had also established strategic connections within Parliament. For example, the important Safeguarding Committee of the House of Commons (responsible in the 1920s for any protectionist measures imposed) was under the chairmanship of Colonel Gretton, who was invited to be vice-chairman of EIA and accepted readily. All manner of techniques were adopted in the advancement of propaganda – from the simple financial reward of those who managed to publish letters in the press under their own names advocating protection (2/6d for a letter in the provincial press, 5/- for one in London) to the employment of paid individuals to draft the letters.[51] Other techniques were to use industries looking for protection to finance huge advertising campaigns. One such operation was carried out with Bryant and May.[52].

There were also requests initiated by British industry for assistance. A letter from the British Brush Manufacturers asked if the EIA could assist them in pressing their application for a safeguarding Order. Given that Colonel Gretton was vice-chairman of one organisation and chairman of the other it must be regarded as obvious that they could, and did, though conclusive evidence is not available. At the same time, the British Film Committee invited the cooperation of the Association in their campaign on British films.[53]

The interesting question that remains is why, when most countries had tariffs and nominal levels were being raised, did Britain not have a tariff sooner? The simple answer is, of course, that free trade attitudes were deeply ingrained in the British consciousness. An important aspect of this was the belief, originating in the nineteenth century, in cheap food. Food came in large part from Empire and the markets for British manufactured goods were increasingly in Empire countries. In order to secure these markets and enlarge them something had to be done in Britain to reciprocate with preference for Empire primary producers. The loudest cries from the latter were for tariffs on foreign food in order that a preference could be extended to Empire. This was a stumbling block to protection, for the British electorate associated protection with dearer food and no assurance was forthcoming that dearer food would not result. The fact was that no assurance could be given so long as manufacturers needed Empire support. It is nevertheless surprising that more attention was not given to this problem difficult though it was. It was the middle of 1931 before the EIA considered the question of producing 'Literature dealing with the "Dear Food" cry',[54] by which time of course the tariff was close to a certainty.

The argument thus far then has been that the British rejection of free trade principles that had been adhered to for almost eighty years cannot be explained simply as a result of economic depression. Equally while political factors played their part, the origins of the tariff are better understood in terms of a fairly consistent pressure from domestic industry that emerged in the First World War and gained more adherents in the course of the next decade. The economic experience of the 1920s reinforced, for important parts of industry, the mood that had developed during the First World War. Awareness of the activities of pressure groups and the potential damage that could result from unrestrained activities of tariff seekers led governments to devise some means of diffusing, if not eliminating, the pressure it was likely to be subjected to. The decision to impose a uniform general tariff was government's but, in order to escape from the responsibility of adjusting the structure, an independent body was created. That is the subject of the next chapter.

Notes

1   M. W. Beresford, *The Leeds Chamber of Commerce* (1951), p. 108.
2   A good account of this is provided in Benjamin H. Brown, *The Tariff Reform Movement in Great Britain, 1881–1895* (1943).
3   *The Times*, 22 July 1903. Morrison shows how Chamberlain was committed to economic motives as well in A. J. Morrison, 'The Development of a Tariff Reform Policy during Joseph Chamberlain's First Campaign' in W. H. Challoner and Barrie M. Ratcliffe (eds), *Trade and Transport* (1977).
4   A. W. Coats, 'Political Economy and the Tariff Reform Campaign of 1903', *Journal of Law and Economics* (1968).
5   Brown, op. cit., Preface.
6   E. B. McGuire, *The British Tariff System* (1951), p. 242.
7   *British Parliamentary Papers*, 1918, *Final Report of the Committee on Commercial and Industrial Policy After the War*, Cd 9035, p. 46.
8   ibid., p. 52.
9   The concept of the effective rate of protection and some measures of it for the British economy in the 1930s can be found in Chapter 8.
10 *Iron and Coal Trade Review*, 24 March 1916.
11 *British Parliamentary Papers, 1918, Report of the Departmental Committee on Iron and Steel After the War.* Cd 9071.
12 ibid., p. 29.
13 ibid.
14 ibid.

15   *The British Iron and Steel Federation* (1963).
16   R. K. Snyder, *The Tariff Problem in Great Britain, 1918–1923* (1944).
17   Wedgwood Benn highlighted the absurdity of the 'pivotal' industry notion by pointing out that busts for corset modelling were included in the list of key industries, *Parliamentary Debates*, 5th Series, Vol. 141, Cols 1610–12.
18   Snyder, op.cit.
19   Public Record Office, CAB 24/224, CP 278.
20   Committee on Iron and Steel Industries, Public Record Office, CAB 58/127–131.
21   See Chapter 8.
22   Public Record Office, CAB 58/128.
23   Public Record Office, CAB 58/129.
24   Public Record Office, CAB 58/127 and evidence presented to the Balfour Committee in December 1924 and October 1925.
25   Public Record Office, CAB 58/128, CR (I & S) 28.
26   Public Record Office, CAB 58/129, CR (I & S) 33.
27   Robert Self, 'Tariffs and Conservative Party 1922–1931' (PhD Thesis, LSE 1980).
28   This is the approach found in K. W. D. Rolf, 'Tories Tariffs and Elections: The West Midlands in English Politics 1918–35' (unpublished PhD Thesis, Cambridge, 1974).
29   A recent example is found in Tom Traves, *The State and Enterprise: Canadian Manufacturers and the Federal Government, 1917–1931* (1979).
30   Andrew Roth, *The Business Background of Members of Parliament* (1959).
31   Speech at Liverpool; see *Manchester Guardian*, 9 January 1932.
32   Rolf, op.cit., p. 254.
33   Quoted in Ronald M. Findlay, *Britain under Protection* (1934), p. 108.
34   W. A. S. Hewins, *Trade in the Balance* (1924).
35   *The Economist*, 25 December 1915, p. 1061.
36   J. A. Turner, 'The British Commonwealth Union and the General Election of 1918', *English Historical Review* (1978).
37   *The Times*, 27 April 1921.
38   A. J. P. Taylor, *English History 1914–45* (1965), p. 208.
39   ibid., p. 207.
40   Robert Rhodes James, *Memoirs of a Conservative: J. C. C. Davidson's Memoirs and Papers 1910–37* (1969), p. 182.
41   John Ramsden, *The Age of Balfour and Baldwin 1902–40* (1978), p. 297.
42   L. C. S. Amery, *My Political Life*, Vol. II (1953–5), p. 291.
43   ibid., Vol. III (1955), p. 80.
44   *Empire Industries Association (EIA)*, Executive Committee Minutes, 15 July 1925.
45   *Hannon Papers* (House of Lords), Box 17, Folder 1.
46   *EIA*, 22 September 1925. He did, however, appear at later meetings and played some active part.
47   *EIA*, 22 July 1925. The general meetings were well attended and as one indication of the business connections of the group, of 78 attending the meeting on 25 November 1931, 40 are listed as directors of companies in the 1931 *Directory of Directors*.
48   *EIA*, Minutes, General Meeting, 3 August 1926.
49   ibid.
50   *Beaverbrook Papers* (House of Lords), BBK C/5, 12 November 1928.
51   *EIA*, Executive Minutes, 7 April 1925 and 5 July 1927.
52   ibid., 1 June 1927.
53   ibid., 17 February 1927.
54   ibid., 9 June 1931.

6

Determining the Tariff Structure

Most tariff theory has suggested that any tariff is irrational, apart from the infant industry argument and that of the optimum tariff. Recently this has changed, and there are several explanations that can be considered, particularly when seeking to say something about the shape of tariff structures.

This chapter examines factors important in shaping the British tariff structure of the early 1930s. For the purposes of this examination, the effective tariff rate should provide a better representation of the tariff structure than the nominal rate. The effective rate of protection gives expression to the margin of protection on value-added in the production process rather than simply that on the product price.[1] It shows by how much value-added in the industry can exceed the value-added in the absence of protection. Now empirical studies for various countries and different periods generally make the point that effective rates are roughly one and a half to two times as high as nominal rates. It may be wondered, then, what point there is in using such a structure in preference to the nominal tariff structure. If effective rates were uniformly twice as high there would indeed be no point in differentiating between the two structures. However there are several differences for Britain in this period of sufficient size to make it worthwhile to test both structures, and the results vindicate this decision.

There was a widespread underlying appreciation on the part of businessmen that the rate of protection that mattered to them was the effective rate, though it was not articulated as such. This of course had long been the case,[2] and there are many contemporary remarks of the kind ' . . . the bootmakers . . . being an organised and wealthy trade, they would doubtless make sufficient noise to prevent the tanners from getting a duty'.[3]

Tariff-making bodies have also long had an understanding of the effective rate. For example, the Import Duties Advisory Committee tried to allow for it in making the tariff:

the schedule covers by far the greater part of the manufactured products now being imported into this country... We have... excluded many commodities on special grounds, for example, on account of their importance to other industries...[4]

Three possible influences on the tariff structure are considered. The first has its basis in the belief that government has a separate welfare function that sees political gain in a device that redistributes income towards groups with some political clout; the effect, however, is obscure to the more numerous losers. The second is that some explanation may lie in the large regional differences in the British economy in both production and factor markets between the wars. Finally, given a 'conservative' welfare function, it may be justifiable to provide protection for industries under severe import pressure. The chapter proceeds as follows. First, these hypotheses are examined. Secondly, there is a description of the measures used in testing the hypotheses. Finally, the results are presented and discussed. More than the customary caution about the data is required, for there are numerous deficiencies. At the appropriate place in the discussion these will be pointed out.

Influences on the Tariff Structure

Industrial pressure
Several politico-economic models have recently been advanced in order to explain tariff structures.[5] Drawing as they do on economic and political theory, these models furnish a number of hypotheses that are potentially useful in a consideration of the making of the general tariff in Britain.

Applications of most of these models are found in the literature on North America and there are essential differences of political and historical character between the United States and the United Kingdom that deserve comment. The first is that the United States has a long tariff history, and interested economic groups were better acquainted than their British counterparts with the potential gains and losses involved in tariff adjustment, and more accustomed to lobbying for gain. More than this they were readier to participate in, and had greater facility for participating in, the tariff-making process. For example, Pincus has shown how, in the early nineteenth century, interested groups petitioned Congress over the tariff.[6] Such activity continued throughout the nineteenth century and down to 1929 when tariff revisions were under consideration in the Hawley–Smoot bill. In 1929 public hearings were conducted. These public hearings are of critical importance in the course of a bill through Congress for it is here that Congress invites and shapes the pressures to which it is subjected; and the hearings define and formulate the questions on which Congress debates. In 1929, in response to the public notice given on the hearings, more than 1100 persons sought a hearing before the Ways and Means Committee and a similar number applied to the Committee on Finance.[7] Clearly the opportunities for sophisticated pressure groups to operate were plentiful. Coupled with this of course is the greater allegiance an American Senator has to his constituency and a correspondingly lesser allegiance to his party than the British Member of Parliament.

One approach of political economy to the tariff is what has been called by Caves the 'adding machine' model.[8] The postulation here is that governments act to maximise the probability of their re-election and in so doing they present a bundle of policies to the elector that they believe will attract the greatest number of votes.[9] The link between this approach and the tariff structure lies in the effect of tariffs on income distribution. The tariff changes the distribution of factor incomes, and political parties try to assess the effect of anticipated changes on political support. It was felt, however, that empirical testing of this notion in the framework of the Heckscher–Ohlin model should not be attempted. Too many uncertainties arise over factor intensiveness, and even where theoretical difficulties can be surmounted the measures available for testing are too frail to allow any useful conclusions. In any case, it seems more realistic in the circumstances to expect that tariffs affect incomes only in the protected industries themselves, and to accept that, because of comparative factor immobility, gains to producers would not be dispersed by competition through the economy. But a given tariff generally hurts the consumer and benefits the producers, and since the voting power of the consumer is greater than that of the producer (though the former may be scattered and the latter concentrated) the question is, why should a vote-maximising government ever propose a new tariff or raise an existing one? The answer may be that an industry can offer immediate support to political parties whereas consumers may be slow in grasping the cost to themselves.

The most successful of the models in terms of explanatory power tend to be of the 'interest group' type. These suggest that tariff rates (either nominal or effective) are the result of interest group pressures and should depend on the structural factors controlling the benefits and costs for industry groups. Interest group considerations predict a positive relation between tariffs and industrial size (or perhaps seller concentration) partly because of the ability of large concentrated industries to use excess profits, or simply influence, for lobbying activities. Against this, of course, an industry's ability to secure

protection suffers if those harmed by its protection are able to organise efficiently to oppose it. The incentive for an industry to act
would depend on the expected net increase in profits (or utility).

Pressure groups of all kinds had been active in British political life
in the early twentieth century and of course groups working for
protection were quite strong at the turn of the century.

British industrialists, as we have seen, certainly took to pro-
tectionist ideas increasingly in the 1920s and with such alacrity in the
later years of the decade that they were almost unanimous by 1930.
There is evidence, too, that lobbying activities were prevalent in
Britain in the 1920s and that the British were as aware as the
Americans of the dangers of log-rolling.[10]

There are also indications that lobbying was successful in Britain
in the 1920s. For example, the chairman of Messrs Grout & Co. Ltd
(silk manufacturers), addressing shareholders at the annual general
meeting in the late 1920s, said:

> We started a very vigorous campaign inside the House of Com-
> mons with a view to impressing upon the Chancellor of the Ex-
> chequer the vital importance of doing something for our industry.
> It is common knowledge that our efforts were crowned with some
> measure of success.[11]

There are many other such examples. Persistent pressure by some
industries had already secured some protection, as we have noted.
Other industries, while unsuccessful in their quest for duties in the
1920s (for example iron and steel), had been presenting their
respective cases throughout that decade, and others again had been
resisting them. This pressure probably confirmed the Conservatives
in their pursuit of protection in the late 1920s, or convinced them of
the fact that a protectionist policy would be successful at the polls.
When the National Government was formed in 1931 (at which time
there had been considerable activity by interested groups working
for a protectionist victory) it was dominated by Conservatives and it
was then widely accepted that a tariff would be introduced.

The Abnormal Importations Act was passed in November 1931. It
was said to be an emergency measure and gave some manufacturers
protective duties of 50 per cent. In February 1932 these duties were
removed in the legislation that provided the general tariff of 10 per
cent. It was the declared intention of the British government to
endeavour to keep the tariff out of politics and it therefore created
an 'independent and neutral body' (the Import Duties Advisory
Committee) to make recommendations on tariff revision to the
Board of Trade. The great bulk of revisions were carried through in
1932, though several amendments were made in each of the years

following. A member of the Committee wrote at the end of the 1930s:

> Clearly the principles underlying the tariff must remain a political
> issue; the Government could not divest itself of responsibility for
> them; but it was felt to be desirable that in the detailed application of
> the principles so determined there should be no scope for the kind of
> political activity known elsewhere as 'lobbying' or 'parliamentary
> log-rolling' . . . It is, I think, proper to put on record in this place that
> from the time it came into being until the outbreak of the present
> war . . . its refusal from the first to entertain representations from
> persons or organisations other than those having immediate interest
> in matters before it made it equally free from any kind of political
> pressure.[12]

In other words, in 1932 the circumstances under which lobbying might
take place were changed. As D. N. Chester put it:

> The political problems can prove even more difficult. For differen-
> tial tariffs create interests, and these lead to pressure groups and
> lobbies. The amount at stake in terms of profitability, employment,
> and earnings may be quite large. No effort is likely to be spared in
> presenting the case formally, and there are obvious temptations to
> use political contacts to secure a favourable decision.
>   The Import Duties Advisory Committee was the administrative
> device used to tackle these problems.[13]

It is worth looking in a little detail at the structure and work of the
Import Duties Advisory Committee. The Committee comprised a
chairman and between two and five other members appointed by the
Treasury. It had the power to require any person to give information or
appear as witness before it. Responsibility for imposing or removing
customs duties remained in the hands of the House of Commons but it
appears that the House always accepted the recommendations of the
Committee. The procedure followed by the IDAC on the receipt of an
application was, firstly, to gather relevant information on the case and
then to interview or correspond with the applicant, clarifying or
supplementing the application. If the committee was satisfied that a
prima facie case was made, the application was advertised in the *Board
of Trade Journal*, the daily press and the appropriate trade periodicals.
For instance, the following notice appeared in the *Board of Trade
Journal*:

> The Import Duties Advisory Committee give notice of the following
> applications for the imposition of increased duties:

By the British Hacksaw Makers' Association in respect of Hack-
saws.

. . .

Any representations which interested parties desire to make in
regard to these commodities should be addressed in writing to the
Secretary (IDAC) . . . not later than June 20th.[14]

Those opposed to the requested tariff revision were then given an
opportunity of commenting (though not a lot of time to prepare);
their case in turn was sent back to the applicant for a rejoinder. There
might be a meeting of applicant and opponents, though these were
not held in public.[15] According to Ashley, this method of tariff
making and revision had no parallel in any other country.[16]

It should be clear from this brief description of procedure that
scope for applying pressure, if it existed, was of a wholly different
kind from that in the United States. Of course there would have been
opportunities for applicant and opponent to bargain without know-
ledge of the Committee and for opponents to encourage other potential users to make representations to the Committee. The wool and
worsted industry provides an example of an industry that used considerable pressure – besieging its MPs, government departments and
the Committee itself. Hutchinson, Secretary to the Committee,
claims that the Committee was not open to such pressure, especially
from MPs, and while we should be wary of such a claim from a
member of the Committee, this does appear to be a reasonable
assessment.[17]

Sir Arthur Salter wrote at this time:

After several years of trying to get into the minds of those who
were nominally in control of commercial policies, I came to the
conclusion that the secret calculation in most minds was one of the
strengths of political groups and political pressures on the Government. Nearly all of them were habitually thinking in terms not of
the economic policy which they considered, rightly or wrongly, the
best for their country, but in terms of the reactions of any given
policy upon the groupings of parties and sections on which their
political support depended.

and he continued:

. . . . . the operative principle underlying the flexible varied and
changeable system is . . . that those interests which are so organised
as to exercise the strongest political pressure get protection or the

highest rates of protection at the expense of the rest of the community.[18]

Salter, however, was writing of his experience of several European countries, in the course of the 1920s. The suggestion is, then, that the conditions for lobbying, and its practice, were prevalent in Britain in the 1920s, but that in 1932 the procedure set up for shaping the tariff did greatly lessen the possibility of pressure being exerted even if it did not remove it altogether.

The variable normally used to capture political clout is size or market power. The first part of the proposition to be tested is the relationship between market power, as measured by the degree of 'concentration' (i.e. the extent to which large firms dominate the industry), and the effective tariff. The usual hypothesis is that a powerful lobby should derive from a highly concentrated industry and that the success of the lobby can be gauged from the levels of either nominal or effective tariff rates secured. The argument here is that this was not the case for Britain in the 1930s. Further, it is probable that oligopolies were *less* likely to cooperate, being notoriously suspicious groups and more likely to be wary of each other in the information-gathering and presenting exercise. This would have been particularly the case in view of the nature of the material requested by the IDAC: details of sales, prices and costs. The indications are that this is borne out in IDAC hearings.

Indeed the argument goes further. With the danger of pressure removed, the least concentrated industries (in all probability the most needy) should have obtained the greatest protection. Large concentrated industries should be in less need of protection. In terms of the regression equation, a negative sign and a small coefficient should therefore be anticipated.

Regional Pressure

The second area of explanation is the regional one. Again other studies have suggested, for varying reasons, that a high degree of regional concentration of industry would produce the kind of environment most likely to secure action. For example, Pincus shows in his study of America in the early nineteenth century that the intensity of pressure group activity depended on geographical dispersion because of the costs of obtaining information.[19] Clearly in interwar Britain this is not the same kind of consideration. The argument for Britain in the 1930s is twofold. First, as was argued for industry, the possibilities for lobbying were limited because of the nature of the tariff-making process. The IDAC did nevertheless explicitly promote cooperation in the presentation of an application: 'Any application had to be submitted in writing, preferably by an association or group of persons representing a substantial proportion of the trades concerned.'[20] And Hutchinson records that IDAC 'did not refuse to consider representations from individual firms, but it lost no opportunity of encouraging the members of any industry or section of an industry to make a united approach'.[21] An industry that was clustered geographically would have found it easier to pursue, and present, a united case; an industry thinly dispersed across the country was unlikely to possess sufficient cohesion to promote its interests effectively. More than this, the political climate in Britain between the wars was such that anything designed to alleviate the regional difficulties of the time was more likely to gain a sympathetic hearing. In terms of the statistical testing, a positive sign on the regional coefficient should therefore be expected.

Import Pressure
The rate of growth of imports has commonly been held to be an important influence on tariff formation. The highest rates of protection, it is suggested, are conferred on those industries suffering most from foreign competition in the domestic market. Indeed, according to the record of events published by the secretary of the Import Duties Advisory Committee, this was the prime consideration in the 1930s when an application was examined: 'The first point to be considered in examining an application for a higher duty was the extent of imports, their growth, and their relation to the home output.'[22] There are two elements present here: the first is concerned simply with the rate of growth of imports and the second with the relationship between imports and domestic output.

The 1920s decade was not one of flourishing British trade, though some products fared better than others. In both value and volume terms differing experience is found, there being rises and falls in imports of various commodities between the years 1924 and 1930. Amongst those that increased most in value were electrical engineering goods (108.3 per cent) and timber products (62.7 per cent). The biggest falls were recorded in roofing felt (62.5 per cent) and motor vehicles (53.5 per cent). Iron and steel imports grew just a little in value terms, by 4.5 per cent. Few quantity figures are available for comparison but where they are, for example for the iron and steel industry, there do not appear to have been 'excessive' imports. For one of the major groupings (blooms, billets and slabs) there was a fall of 19.6 per cent between these years. As far as the whole range of industries goes, a comparison of the change in imports between 1924 and 1930 on the twenty-three items available with the appropriate effective rates provides a very poor rank correlation coefficient. That is, the growth of imports of itself appears to have been very poorly related, if at all, to the effective tariff structure. The more potent version of the argument concerns the relation between imports and domestic activity. And it is the measure that best captures this that is used in the formal test.

This discussion of the variables and their degree of association has argued that the effective tariff structure is the most appropriate dependent variable and that measures of industrial size, regional clustering and import competition should all be included as the most important elements in the explanation of that structure. The following relationship therefore is the one to be tested:

$$T_e = f(S, R, F)$$

where T_e = effective tariff structure
S = size concentration of industry
R = regional concentration of industry
F = a measure of import competition

What follows is an account of the actual measures employed and how they 'performed' in the regression equations.

Testing the Hypotheses

The first measure considered is that of size. High levels of concentration are often thought to be a fairly new phenomenon, but recent studies have shown that the 1920s in Britain witnessed the greatest growth of mergers in any decade in this century before the 1960s, and that the degree of concentration in British manufacturing industry in 1930 (as captured in this instance by the market share of the 100 largest firms) was higher than at any time between 1900 and the 1950s.[23]

For the purposes of this exercise, there are many measures that might be used to examine concentration and there are several indicators of size that might be selected. Most measures of concentration, however, have been attacked on some grounds and data constraints did not allow much choice. For example, the Herfindahl measure appeared to be unduly biased by the class intervals of the census data and a concentration ratio of the top ten firms could not be extracted from the data. In any case it has been shown that most measures of size follow each other quite closely and no great violence is done by the selection of one rather than another. Equally, the form in which the variable is expressed is not of crucial importance. For example, there is little difference in the ranking of concentration by gross output, net output or number of employees. The measures of concentration employed here were the employment of labour (CMET) con-

Table 6.1 *Measures of Concentration in British Industry, 1930*

		Size concentration		Regional concentration[3]		
		CMET[1]	CNOT[2]	RCP	RCV	RCE
1	Iron & Steel Manufacturing	.55	.57	.22	.17	.17
2	Motor Vehicles	.70	.73	.30	.46	.48
3	Electrical Engineering	.69	.71	.34	.33	.32
4	Timber Trades	.40	.42	.22	.31	.27
5	Cotton Spinning & Doubling	.36	.40	.80	.74	.80
6	Cotton Weaving	.35	.35	.83	.87	.90
7	Chemicals	.60	.59	.22	.17	.24
8	Woollen & Worsted	.42	.42	.67	.61	.62
9	Non-ferrous Metals	.47	.49	.33	.30	.34
10	Shipbuilding	.60	.60	.17	.25	.24
11	Boot & Shoe	.47	.48	.22	.25	.24
12	Furniture	.41	.43	.27	.39	.33
13	Silk	.68	.75	.28	.31	.30
14	Rubber	.63	.71	.39	.34	.32
15	Soap, Candles, Perfumery	.64	.64	.32	.43	.41
16	Tramways & Light Rail	.44	.44	.22	.32	.32
17	Paint, Colour, Varnish	.43	.47	.27	.30	.31
18	Railway Carriage & Wagon	.59	.60	.18	.26	.28
19	Glass	.62	.64	.24	.27	.24
20	Building Materials	.20	.22	.18	.24	.23
21	China & Earthenware	.37	.34	.68	.73	.79
22	Hat & Cap	.42	.40	.36	.48	.48
23	Lace	.37	.33	—	—	—
24	Fur	.32	.28	.70	.81	.79
25	Glove	.33	.29	.42	.53	.62
26	Manufacturing Abrasives	.40	.37	.51	.51	.57
27	Roofing Felt	.18	.19	1.0	1.0	1.0
28	Umbrella	.39	.33	.35	.35	.32

[1] the share of employment controlled by the top 10 per cent of firms.
[2] the share of net output produced by the top 10 per cent of firms.
[3] measure used is the Herfindahl.
Source: calculated from *Census of Production*, 1930.
Note: All these measures of concentration should be regarded as approximate. The *Census of Production* (1930) excluded all firms employing ten people or less, but our calculation has left this out of account. Some industries would clearly be more affected by this than others.

trolled by the top 10 per cent of firms and the share of net output (CNOT) produced by the top 10 per cent of firms. Table 6.1 presents the measures calculated. The first measure can be seen to have a range of .18 to .70 and to be fairly evenly spread. The second measure shows only slight variation from the first.

Table 6.1 also provides the measure of regional concentration used. That measure was the Herfindahl ratio and it was possible to calculate Herfindahl ratios using three different variables: the number of establishments in a particular industry in a region (RCP), the number of employees in that industry in a region (RCE) and the net output of that industry per region (RCV). The range of the measure is .17 to 1.00 and all three are highly correlated.[24] The

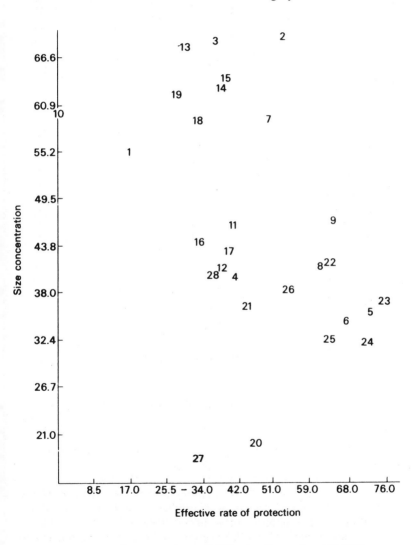

Figure 6.1a   Concentration and Effective Protection (CMET)

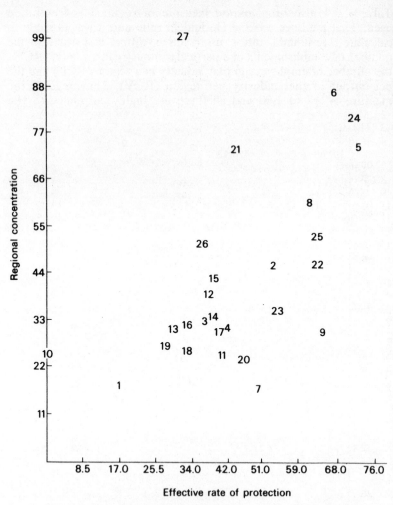

Figure 6.1b   Concentration and Effective Protection (RCV)

regions are the eleven industrial regions in the United Kingdom as defined by the 1930 *Census of Production*.

Figure 6.1 is a scatter diagram for both the size and regional concentration measures derived, plotted with the effective rate of protection. The industries are numbered as in Table 6.1 and it can be seen that there is a fairly pronounced negative slope for the size measure and a positive one for the regional measure, supporting the anticipated signs of the coefficients already discussed.

Table 6.2 *Measures of Import Penetration*

		Percentage change in value of imports, 1924–30	Percentage change in imports as share of domestic output, 1924–30
1	Iron & Steel Manufacturing	4.5	30.7
2	Motor Vehicles	−53.5[1]	−191.0
3	Electrical Engineering	108.3	63.3
4	Timber Trades	62.7	41.1
5	Cotton Spinning & Weaving	4.6	132.0
7	Chemicals	−7.2	0.0
8	Woollen & Worsted	3.8	75.8
9	Non-ferrous Metals	18.9	−30.1
11	Boot & Shoe	6.5	14.3
12	Furniture	55.1	19.1
13	Silk	−38.8	46.1
14	Rubber	−13.6	200.0
15	Soap, etc.	19.1	31.7
17	Paint, etc.	22.3	10.2
19	Glass	16.8	10.5
21	China	27.2	53.5
22	Hat & Cap	71.4	85.2
23	Lace	3.6[2]	28.1
24	Fur	20.9	58.8
25	Glove	−42.9	−56.9
26	Manufacturing Abrasives	3.0	−12.2
27	Roofing Felt	−62.5	−65.4
28	Umbrella	63.0	36.4

[1] duty imposed in 1925.
[2] duty imposed 30 June 1930.
Source: calculated from the *Trade and Navigation Accounts* and *Census of Production*, 1924 and 1930.

There are several ways of measuring import penetration and they have all been used in empirical work.[25] One is to relate the value of imports in a particular industry to that industry's final output. A second is to relate the value of imports to the value of domestic sales. And a third approach is to deal in a measure of quantity and relate the number of units imported to the number of units of domestic sales. This last measure is clearly appropriate only for a single product market. In most empirical studies the second measure has been more commonly employed, though for the purposes of this exercise it presents difficulties. Use of it means that the import penetration ratio depends not only on imports and domestic output but also on exports. Indeed, an increase in exports *ceteris paribus* would raise the

Table 6.3 Concentration and the Tariff Structure: Regression Results

		Intercept							$\bar{R}^2$
(1)	ER =	55.754 (3.229)	−	0.517 CMET (1.975)	+	0.358 RCP (1.647)	+	0.032 DM (0.504)	.5550
(2)	ER =	52.113 (2.967)	−	0.468 CMET (1.768)	+	0.348 RCE (2.034)	+	0.046 DM (0.810)	.5738
(3)	ER =	56.700 (3.690)	−	0.512 CNOT (2.310)	+	0.310 RCP (1.613)	+	0.056 DM (0.858)	
(4)	ER =	53.572 (3.401)	−	0.472 CNOT (2.099)	+	0.304 RCP (1.782)	+	0.066 DM (1.139)	.6041
(5)	NR =	20.334 (2.402)	+	0.005 CMET (0.037)	+	0.089 RCP (0.938)	−	0.024 DM (0.776)	.1099
(6)	NR =	15.735 (1.900)	+	0.006 CMET (0.499)	+	0.132 RCE (1.636)	−	0.028 DM (1.035)	.0174
(7)	NR =	22.582 (2.886)	−	0.030 CNOT (0.266)	+	0.070 RCP (0.721)	−	0.020 DM (0.606)	.1040
(8)	NR =	18.206 (2.344)	+	0.022 CNOT (0.198)	+	0.117 RCE (1.396)	−	0.026 DM (0.920)	.0016
(9)	ER =	48.365 (3.222)	−	0.347 CMET (1.531)	+	0.402 RCP (2.822)			.4642
(10)	ER =	42.437 (2.788)	−	0.281 CMET (1.251)	+	0.421 RCE (3.185)			.5017
(11)	ER =	45.891 (3.455)	−	0.296 CNOT (1.560)	+	0.408 RCP (2.923)			.4663
(12)	ER =	39.885 (2.888)	−	0.229 CNOT (1.200)	+	0.427 RCE (3.236)			.4989

(13)	NR	=	25.867 (3.317)	−	0.014 CMET (0.115)	−	0.032 RCP (0.434)	.0843
(14)	NR	=	17.619 (2.177)	+	0.076 CMET (0.635)	+	0.061 RCE (0.865)	.0564
(15)	NR	=	28.050 (4.078)	−	0.046 CNOT (0.477)	−	0.046 RCP (0.633)	.0733
(16)	NR	=	20.891 (2.823)	+	0.023 CNOT (0.228)	+	0.044 RCE (0.062)	.0740

Statistics are given in brackets beneath the coefficients and constants.

ER = effective tariff rate
NR = nominal tariff rate
CMET = size concentration (employment)
CNOT = size concentration (net output)
RCP = regional concentration (plant)
RCV = regional concentration (net output)
RCE = regional concentration (employment)
DM = import penetration

import penetration ratio and a decrease in exports would reduce it. The best guide to import penetration in our case would seem to be obtained by using the first measure, where the ratio rises as imports increase relative to domestic output. Furthermore this is closest to what the IDAC claims to have been guided by. Table 6.2 presents both the change in value of imports and the first measure of import penetration. This shows that for some products the ratio fell, for some it rose considerably and for others it remained stable. Iron and steel imports as a percentage of total domestic output rose by 30.7 per cent between 1924 and 1930 and this was the median in the list of twenty-three products, whose range was fairly wide – −191.0 per cent to +200 per cent.

Emphasis must be given to the immense difficulties of matching *Trade and Navigation Account* data with *Census of Production* data. Sometimes these difficulties are insurmountable,[26] and it was not always possible to make even a rough assessment of the degree of import penetration for an industry. The IDAC of course faced the same problem when making their calculation, and, while they recognised that whatever method was adopted presented difficulties – 'The other alternative, so far as industrial products are concerned is to proceed on the basis of information which has been collected by the Board of Trade in recent years . . . we fully recognise that it will involve mistakes and omissions'[27] – it does seem that they were often content to accept figures provided by the applicants themselves.[28]

Results

Turning to the results of the regression analysis, from the argument presented in the first section of this chapter we should expect the regression equation to produce a negative sign on the 'size' coefficient and positive signs on the other two coefficients. Table 6.3 presents the regression results for the equation $T_e = a + b_1 S + b_2 R + B_3 - F$, and for a similar test of the nominal tariff structure.

The first point of interest to emerge from the table is that, in terms of statistical significance, the equations with the nominal rate of protection as the dependent variable ((5)–(8)) are so weak as to be worth no further consideration, save to reinforce the point that the nominal tariff structure is not the one that mattered; no reliable coefficient and no level of explanation is offered in the equations. The equations with the effective rates ((1)–(4)) are quite different and confirm that it was the effective tariff structure that mattered to policy makers. In all cases the predicted sign is obtained and in most cases the coefficients for the 'size' and 'regional' variables are significant. The only disappointing feature is that the measure of import penetration (DM) has a both very low and far from significant co-efficient and therefore contributes nothing to the explanation.

Since the import penetration variable never performed very well, and further since its inclusion reduced the number of observations that could be used, it was dropped from the equation and the regression re-run. Equations (9)–(16) present the results of this latter exercise. A very similar set of results is obtained for the nominal tariff (equations (13)–(16)), which is again shown to be inappropriate and of no further interest. In the other equations ((9)–(12)), the 'regional' coefficient gains in statistical significance while the 'size' coefficient loses. It is possible that some multicollinearity exists between the regional measure and the import penetration measure, but this is something that would not be readily anticipated, for there is no good reason to suppose that industries suffering the greatest foreign competition would be those with the greatest degree of regional concentration.

These results then confirm the negative relationship between size concentration and the effective tariff structure and the positive relationship between regional concentration and the dependent variable. In other words, industries least concentrated by size got the highest rates of protection.

There are acknowledged weaknesses in this exercise. One is the availability of industries and the manner in which they are grouped together. This could introduce a certain imbalance in that some rather large industries are lumped together with fairly small ones. For analytical purposes some of the large industries should ideally be at a more disaggregated level. Others too would be better disaggregated for other reasons. One such example is the carpet industry, which should be separated from the woollen industry because its international trading experience was wholly different. Unfortunately data limitations prevent this.

Another point that should be stressed is that it cannot be argued from the sign on the 'size' variable that small industries were better able to secure protection on grounds such as that this was less likely to affect the cost of living, because the size variable is a measure of concentration. It does not refer to absolute size. Indeed, when absolute size was tested no significant results were produced. That is to say, neither the infant industry argument nor anything associated with it is behind this result. The argument that the least concentrated by size would have been the most needy and therefore most likely to secure higher protection can be supported to some extent by reference to the mood of the time, which was to encourage concentration – though the term used was rationalisation. The outstanding example of this was the iron and steel industry where the bargain made between the IDAC and the industry was that greater protection would be granted in exchange for evidence of rationalisation.[29]

It has been frequently argued, particularly in recent years, that unemployment is the chief consideration in the making of a tariff and it may be that the regional explanation contains an element of this, given that unemployment in the 1920s and 1930s was heavily concentrated in several regions. Some attempt, albeit feeble, was made at alleviating regional distress in this period and unemployment was one of the declared concerns. So it could be that a political climate favoured a sympathetic hearing to applications from badly affected areas.

One other point that can be made here is that it is sometimes suggested that higher rates of protection should be given to those goods nearest to the final consumer since this would hurt intermediaries least. We have already noted that the IDAC was concerned over this. And it is interesting to note that the Federation of British Industries prepared an emergency tariff scheme in 1931, the guiding principle of which was that the nearer a commodity was to a finished good the higher the rate of duty it should bear.[30] However, this is already allowed for if we accept that it was the effective rate that influenced decisions, since the smaller the value-added (i.e. the nearer to a finished good) the greater is the effective protection provided.

In summary, then, it has been hypothesised that the effective tariff rates provide the most satisfactory description of the tariff structure, and this seems justified. Further, the results bear out the hypothesis that industry size captured in a concentration ratio provides a suitable surrogate of 'political clout' but that because of the method of tariff-making devised (the setting up of the IDAC, etc.) the effect of such clout was minimised. Moreover, because the least concentrated industries were likely to be in greater need of protection, a negative relationship was predicted and observed. Geographical concentration was a positive influence on the tariff structure because regionally concentrated industries provided the basis for greater cohesion, plus the fact that regional problems were sympathetically received. Although the IDAC claimed to view severe import competition as a primary consideration, there is little support for this in the results, though in view of the data deficiencies of this measure it may have been improper to subject it to the regression analysis and reservations must remain about the role of this variable.

Notes

1 For the calculation of this see Chapter 8.
2 D. C. Coleman provides an example from the beginning of the twentieth century in *Courtaulds: An Economic and Social History* Vol. II (1969), p. 117.

3   A. S. Comyns Carr and D. Rowland Evans, *The Lure of Safeguarding* (1929), p. 23. Within the iron and steel industry the British Steel Re-Rollers Association was formed in 1924 specifically to fight the steelmakers' attempt to obtain duties on imports of semi-products; Public Record Office, CAB 58/128, CR (I & S) 28.

4   *British Parliamentary Papers*, 1931–2, *Recommendations of the Import Duties Advisory Committee*, Cmd 4066, p. 6.

5   Some examples are found in Jonathan J. Pincus, *Pressure Groups and Politics in Antebellum Tariffs* (1977) and J. J. Pincus, 'Pressure Groups and the Pattern of Tariffs', *Journal of Political Economy* (1975); Richard E. Caves, 'Economic Models of Political Choice: Canada's Tariff Structure', *Canadian Journal of Economics* (1976); G. K. Helleiner, 'The Political Economy of Canada's Tariff Structure: An Alternative Model', *Canadian Journal of Economics* (1977).

6   Pincus, *Pressure Groups*, op. cit., Ch. 3.

7   A full description of this is given in E. E. Schattschneider, *Politics, Pressures and the Tariff* (1935).

8   Caves, op.cit.

9   Much of this approach is derived from A. Breton, *The Economic Theory of Representative Government* (1974) and A. Downs, *An Economic Theory of Democracy* (1957).

10 See Chapter 5.

11 Quoted by Ronald M. Findlay in *Britain Under Protection* (1935).

12 Percy Ashley, 'An Experiment in Tariff Making', *Manchester School* (1940), p. 5.

13 Foreword to Sir Herbert Hutchinson, *Tariff-Making and Industrial Reconstruction* (1965).

14 *Board of Trade Journal*, 2 June 1932, p. 786.

15 An outline of the story can be gained from Hutchinson, op.cit., Ch. 2.

16 Ashley, op. cit.

17 The judgement that government was successful in removing the tariff from politics has been made by John S. Eyers, 'Government Direction of Britain's Overseas Trade Policy, 1932–37' (D.Phil. Thesis, 1977), p.ii: 'The intention of the National Government's leaders that the tariff once made should drop out of politics was in the event largely fulfilled.'

18 Sir Arthur Salter, *Recovery* (1933), pp. 179, 183.

19 Pincus, *Pressure Groups*, op.cit., Ch. 5.

20 Ashley, op.cit., p. 22.

21 Hutchinson, op.cit., p. 77.

22 ibid., p. 42.

23 L. Hannah, *The Rise of the Corporate Economy* (1976); Leslie Hannah and J. A. Kay, *Concentration in Modern Industry* (1977), p. 3.

24 The correlation measures are as follows:

$$RCV/RCE - .9856$$
$$RCV/RCP - .9456$$
$$RCE/RCP - .9468$$

25 These are conveniently summarised in James J. Hughes and A. P. Thirlwall, 'Trends and Cycles in Import Penetration in the United Kingdom', *Oxford Bulletin of Economics and Statistics* (1977).

26 Output figures are taken from *Census of Production*, which provides industrial groups. Imports are taken from the *Trade and Navigation Accounts*, which list products.

27 Cmd 4066, op.cit., p. 5, para. 9.

28 Hutchinson, op.cit., pp. 42, 43.

29 J. C. Carr and W. Taplin, *History of the British Steel Industry* (1962), pp. 484–95.

30 *The Times*, 19 September 1931.

7

Some Immediate Economic Effects

In the speech in which Neville Chamberlain, as Chancellor of the Exchequer, introduced the tariff legislation in the House of Commons in February 1932, a defence of the radical policy was that all the economic and political effects would be beneficial: it would strengthen Empire ties and imperial preference, improve bargaining strength with other countries, raise revenue, improve employment, hold down imports, expand exports, insure against a rise in the cost of living following devaluation, and so on.[1] Some of these aspects of the tariff were commented on by contemporaries or have been discussed since by economic and political historians. Most of the investigations have regrettably been of a rather perfunctory kind.

The purpose of this chapter is to examine some of the economic effects of the tariff. First, we look at how protectionism was viewed at the time, as reflected in the serious press and in some of the pamphlet literature. Secondly, we examine some of the more serious assessments of the period, including that of government itself, in an effort to see what effects were either aimed at or hoped for and what was believed to have been achieved. Thirdly, in a brief historiographical survey, we consider the conclusions of economic historians writing on the subject since the Second World War. Finally, the results of an exercise in partial equilibrium analysis are presented in order to indicate some likely effects.

Contemporary Views on Protectionism

As Britain was in the process of changing direction on trade policy, passionate comment came from all quarters. As the pamphlet literature grew, so the outpourings of the press soared. Views ranged from the hasty and ill-considered comment of some sections of the press, including respected monthlies, to more cautious attempts at estimation. The former were frequently propagandist in design and the latter did not altogether escape from the grip of ideology. The range of opinions encompassed a wide field, extending to the view that a British tariff would hasten the growth of fascism in Germany. It was argued that the two countries suffering most from British tariffs were Germany and France and that as a result an entire breakdown was possible in Germany: 'Will the British people take the responsibility for the setting up of a fascist despotism in a Germany, driven to despair?'[2] While in a discussion such as this interactions with the rest of the world cannot be ignored, and far-reaching effects should always be borne in mind, the concern here is first of all with the more direct effects on the British economy.

Those who had supported safeguarding tended to regard it as the principal means of extending protection, and they were of course the keenest demonstrators of its worth. Those who regarded protection as an impediment to economic progress, on the other hand, had no difficulty in finding evidence for their case in the results of the safeguarding duties. It was the ancient game of taking blocks of figures and proving from them whatever might seem to stand in need of proof, allowing the opponent to dispute the accuracy of the figures or the soundness of the conclusion.

On the protectionist side, the claims were simply the opposite of free trade. For example, 'protection ... promotes industrial and political stability ... free trade ... cultivates purely individual and selfish views'[3] – obtained by simply standing Cobden on his head. Support for this position generally took the form: '... employment in 1929 in non-safeguarded industries had risen over 1925 by 5 per cent while employment in safeguarded industries had risen by 25 per cent.'[4] Two authors who claimed that safeguarding had been sufficiently successful to justify its extension were blunt to the point of admitting that protectionists looked at it from the point of view of the producer: 'we can have too many good things at too cheap a price.'[5] A more eloquent account and reasoned case for protection was advanced by a former parliamentary secretary to the Board of Trade, Herbert Williams.[6]

The bulk of the literature, however, was the output of free traders who found forces moving against them. Lord Arnold argued that workers in free trade Britain were better off than those of protectionist Europe, and simply left it at that.[7] Walter Runciman in his most passionate free trade period used a similar technique and pointed to the blast furnaces and rolling mills of Germany and the United States as evidence of the fact that protection had not worked.[8]

When it came to the immediate effects on individual industries there was no shortage of support for protection. On chemicals, J. Davidson Pratt of the Association of the British Chemical Manufacturers wrote: 'The Import Duties Act and increased preferences ...

have improved the position considerably';[9] on iron and steel, Rush wrote: 'largely as a result of the protective tariff ... there has been a definite improvement in the comparative position of the iron and steel industry in the United Kingdom vis-a-vis other countries.'[10] For every casual assertion that the tariff was working there is an equally casual denial.[11]

In the press the least ambiguous and loudest voicing of the protectionist case could be found in the pages of *The Times*, while the free traders had their most effective outlet in *The Economist*. *The Times* had campaigned long for protection and was jubilant over its introduction – it could not refrain from a condemnatory swipe at 'those who had delayed the inevitable change in British policy'. It was confident that the tariff would help British manufacturers to obtain some of the trade that had hitherto been in the hands of foreigners. This enthusiasm for the policy and high expectations for its achievement clouded the paper's judgement when it came to assessing effectiveness. For example, a mere six months after the introduction of the policy *The Times* remarked:

> While it is difficult to estimate exactly the influence of the tariff and the depreciation of sterling in effecting this much needed contraction in imports of inessential commodities, the tariff has probably played the larger part.[12]

For the following twelve months *The Times* contented itself with asserting that the disastrous effects predicted by the opponents of protection had not materialised. A reassertion of its belief in protection came in an assessment of the economy in September 1933, when it firmly put forward the tariff as the chief explanation for recovery:

> In the absence of a general expansion in export business it is clear that the home market has been mainly responsible for the increased absorption of British goods, a development which must in turn be attributed to the benefits derived from the tariff.[13]

The Economist was conceived and born in the heat of the free trade battle almost a century before and it is not too much to say that the preaching of the free trade gospel had been its *raison d'être* ever since. It was of course vehemently opposed to *The Times* and campaigned vigorously against protection in the late 1920s and early 1930s when the threat was becoming pronounced. Possibly as a result of the disappointment suffered in defeat, a mere six weeks after the tariff came into operation *The Economist* arrived at the very hasty judgement that tariffs, together with the depreciation of sterling, had produced no striking change in the balance of payments. Indeed, *The Economist* blamed the poor performance of exports on the barrier that British import restrictions were to the growth of world trade.[14] A month later, *The Economist* had adopted a slightly different stance, claiming that it was impossible to read anything out of the dramatic fall in imports:

> The picture presented by the returns, namely, that of a marked contraction of imports coupled with some slight recovery of exports, has naturally been hailed by our Protectionists as a vindication of their theory. Nothing could be more illusory. It has to be remembered that the trade returns for a particular month represents the results of industrial activity several months earlier.[15]

Ignoring for the moment the rather imperfectly articulated relationship between trade returns and industrial activity, it is obvious that *The Economist* was clutching at straws. An element of confusion had clearly crept into its pages, for it should have been the last to deny that tariffs reduced imports. That is why it was opposed to them. By July it had reverted to a more traditional position, acknowledging that the tariff was doing the job it was designed for. In its *Commercial History and Review of 1932*[16] it remarked that imports had declined much more sharply than exports, due to the introduction of tariffs and the depreciation of sterling.

It must be said, though, that neither of these leaders of the pro and anti factions claimed very much either way for the policy after the middle of 1933, which is just about a year after the introduction of the tariff and less than a full year after its nearly final form had emerged. *The Economist* made this explicit in May of 1933 when it assessed the trade returns and found the suggestion there 'that we are coming to the end of the gold standard and the tariff'.[17] *The Times* simply drifted into other explanations. When it found imports increasing, it put it down to the growth of industrial activity.

Contemporary Assessments of Tariff Legislation

There was one serious study in the 1930s of the immediate effects of the tariff which deserves some attention.[18] It was carried out by H. Leak, a statistician at the Board of Trade, and it set out to establish the production, employment, import and price effects of the tariff for the years 1933 and 1934. For the moment, I shall confine myself to the import reduction effects. Leak's method was to revalue dutiable

Table 7.1   *Reduction in Imports of Dutiable Manufactures, 1933 and 1934*

Rate of duty	Value in 1930	Volume of imports relative to 1930	
	£m.	% 1933	% 1934
20	58	41	48
25	7	59	66
33⅓	17	36	53

Source: H. Leak, 'Some Results of the Import Duties Act', *JRSS*, Pt. IV (1937), p. 569.

manufactures for 1933 and 1934, classified according to the rate of duty, at average values for 1930, taking the corresponding reductions in imports as the effect of the tariff. This procedure produced results of the kind shown in Table 7.1 – in short, a reduction in imports of between 41 per cent and 64 per cent in 1933 and of between 34 per cent and 52 per cent in 1934. Unfortunately these estimates are simply one year's imports compared with another, and we must therefore reject them as being in any sense final. The reduction could be attributed to any number of factors, some of which may well be pulling in different directions. Chief among them may be exchange rate and income effects. Certainly the tariff must be examined, but simply selecting dutiable manufactures does not in any way overcome the difficulty. The usefulness of these estimates may be as starting points in an assessment of all factors, something we shall return to later.

The analysis of those writing in the 1930s focused on the potential the tariff had for correcting the current account deficit and for raising output and employment. As one writer put it:

Indeed protection proved a far greater stimulus to business in the short run than had ever been expected and a considerable proportion of the nation's idle manpower and equipment soon began to find employment in industries which had hitherto failed to make headway against foreign competition under free trade ... The effect of the tariff was to create a wall against foreign competition behind which there automatically accumulated one of the world's largest reservoirs of consuming power.[19]

In other words, by diverting expenditure to domestic goods and raising their price, profits in Britain went up, which led to increasing confidence and investment, and so on. Abel was a wholly committed free trader who poured scorn and sarcasm on protectionists and demonstrated to the satisfaction of all at the Free Trade Union that the tariff was a failure.[20] Benham was more considered. He concluded his investigation of the tariff with the thought that it did assist recovery by stimulating investment in iron and steel and other protected industries. He also believed that employment 'was probably greater than it would have been under free trade' and that the tariff was successful as a bargaining weapon.[21] To Political Economic Planning, a highly respected body, this was not so: 'The British tariff constitutes one of the most important impediments to World Trade which have been created since 1931.'[22]

There were some estimates made by governments of the likely effects of a tariff in the months prior to its introduction. There was of course not much recent experience to draw on, though there was a Cabinet paper prepared in 1931[23] showing the course of employment in industries protected by safeguarding duties over the years 1925–31. While this was used in a suggestive way, it should in fact be wholly rejected as evidence. For one thing, the data were not reliable, having been in all cases but one supplied by the separate manufacturers' associations, occasionally supplemented from outside firms and supported by material from the *Ministry of Labour Gazette*. In the case of one of the principal industries concerned, gas mantles, an international agreement had been reached (and brought into operation at the same time as the duties) that secured the United Kingdom market for United Kingdom manufacturers, and this 'may have exercised an appreciable influence on employment', as the Cabinet paper put it.

More rigorous investigations did take place on the expected outcome of an industrial tariff. In March 1931, when the Labour government was still in power, the Treasury began to give consideration to probable effects, in order to give the government a defence of free trade. From the Treasury, Donald Ferguson wrote to Forber as follows:

> With all the talk that is going around about a 10 per cent revenue tariff I think the Chancellor when he returns will find it necessary to have some ammunition in opposition to the proposal ... what I think would be useful would be up-to-date estimates of the yield on various hypotheses.[24]

Forber replied three weeks later with a long list of estimates, all restricted to the idea of a tariff on imported manufactures. His recommendation was that 'there should be a multiplicity of rates according to the degrees of protection required',[25] thus ignoring the idea of the revenue tariff. But the Treasury was unclear as to what allowance ought to be made for the effect of the tariff on '(a) diminishing the volume of imports and (b) depressing values of the goods still imported' (presumably referring to the terms of trade effects). The strength of its conclusion was therefore that, with retained imports of manufactures at £283m. in 1930, a 10 per cent tax 'might produce (at a guess) £20m. to £32m'.[26] When goods already taxed were excluded, this amount would be reduced to a range of £14–17m.

Economists were, of course, well aware at this time of the elasticity concept, as a statement by Hawtrey to the Macmillan Committee made clear. Hawtrey said that the immediate effect of the tariff would be to raise the price of importables, thus stimulating home production: 'The extent depends in each case on the factor of elasticity.'[27] He assumed for the sake of simplicity that the price elasticity of demand for imports was 1. Hawtrey also felt that the field favourable to protection in British trade was very limited.

Prior to the imposition of the tariff, the government made a more serious attempt at estimating in a partial equilibrium way the likely import and revenue effects of a 10 per cent tariff and a 33⅓ per cent Empire preference. This exercise was carried out by the Customs and Excise Department and presented to the Cabinet in January 1932.[28] The level of disaggregation worked at was that of the Class totals of the *Trade and Navigation Accounts*. Four calculations were made employing different assumptions on which goods were to be included in the tariff and which exempted, and this produced upper and lower bounds for the respective measures.(Table 7.2 draws together the figures used.) The range estimated for the import effect was £33–46m. while that for the revenue effect was £34–58m.

The exercise as presented in the Cabinet Papers is far from detailed, providing simply the bald outlines. However, it allows the calculation of tentative estimates of the implicit price elasticities with which government was operating. For example, the value of goods chargeable together with the estimated reductions anticipated as a result of the duties under Assumption A can be found in Table 7.2. The ratio of Empire imports to foreign imports employed was based on the 1930 import figures (those for 1931 being unavailable);[29] for the various Classes of the *Trade and Navigation Accounts* the ratios were: Class I – 37/63; Class II – 29/71; Class III – 9/91. This is sufficient information to calculate the implicit price elasticities, so long as we assume that the terms of trade and income effects were not allowed for. Since these are nowhere mentioned, it seems fair to proceed on this basis. As far as the terms of trade effect goes, a 10 per cent tariff allowed little scope for any significant effect.

Table 7.2 *Estimated Effects of Tariff under Various Assumptions (£m.)*

	Assumption A[1]			Assumption B[2]			Assumption C[3]			Assumption D[4]		
	Value of goods chargeable	Estimated reduction	Estimated revenue	Value of goods chargeable	Estimated reduction	Estimated revenue	Value of goods chargeable	Estimated reduction	Estimated revenue	Value of goods chargeable	Estimated reduction	Estimated revenue
Class I	168.3	10.8	14.9	316.8	20.2	27.6	182.6	12.2	16.5	182.6	12.2	16.5
Class II	111.7	4.5	9.9	137.9	5.5	12.4	137.9	5.5	12.7	0.0	0.0	0.0
Class III	176.8	19.7	17.2	176.8	19.7	17.2	176.8	19.7	17.2	176.8	19.7	17.2
Other	8.3	0.9	0.7	8.3	0.9	0.7	8.3	0.9	0.7	8.3	0.9	0.7
Total	465.1	35.8	42.7	639.8	46.3	57.9	505.6	37.3	47.1	367.7	32.8	34.4

Sources: compiled from Public Record Office, CAB 27/467, BT (31) 11, and BT (31) 12.

[1] 10 per cent duty with 33⅓ per cent preference on all goods except wheat, meat, tea, cotton, iron ore and goods already dutiable, except under forestalling orders.

[2] 10 per cent duty with 33⅓ per cent preference on all goods except goods already dutiable (other than forestalling orders).

[3] as for B with wheat and meat excluded.

[4] as for C with raw materials also excluded.

Therefore the simple equation that requires solving is:

$$M_e . t_p . n + M_f . t . n = q$$

where M_e = imports from Empire sources
M_f = imports from foreign sources
t_p = preferential tariff rate
t = non-preferential tariff rate
n = price elasticity
q = import reduction

Only n is unknown. By substituting the known values into the equation, the calculation for Class I goods is:

$$(62.3 \times 0.066 \times n) + (106.0 \times 0.1 \times n) = 10.8$$
$$n = .73$$

The results for Classes II and III are obtained in the same way, giving price elasticities of .45 and 1.15 respectively. These parameters agree with theoretical expectations – food (dominating Class I) being price-inelastic (i.e. less than unity) and manufactures being price-elastic (in excess of unity). The magnitudes are also within the limits suggested by other empirical studies and of the size we would have expected to be used. The revenue earnings were presumably then calculated on a similar basis.

The tariff imposed in the first instance actually came closest to Assumption D. Therefore based on these estimates the government was looking for a reduction of £32.8m. on import values overall and securing in addition £34.4m. revenue for the Exchequer. In fact, of course, the tariff imposed on 1 April was raised almost immediately and fairly uniformly to 20 per cent on Class III goods. Reworking these estimates using this figure produces the following results: import reduction, £52.6m.; revenue effect, £44.7m. We must assume that, from the tariff alone, ignoring other restrictive devices such as quantitative restrictions, these figures provided a rough indication of the size of the benefit that government expected to flow.

Indeed, for those inclined to hasty judgement, the experience of the few years following the imposition of the tariff must have provided a vindication of the tariff and a reassuring belief in the forecasting ability of government for, as Table 7.3 shows, the revenue actually collected and to some extent the imports reduced are not wildly different from those predicted after allowance is made for some exchange rate effect. We should however be wary of such a judgement for, as we know, the income effect may well have been substantial.

Table 7.3   *Imports and Revenue, 1930–5 (£m.)*

Class III imports			Revenue		
Year	Total	Fall from 1930	Year	Total	Increase over 1924–31
1930	284	—	Average 1924/5 –30/1	111.7	—
1933	140	144	1932/3	167.2	55.5
1934	160	124	1933/4	179.2	67.5
1935	171	113	1934/5	185.1	73.4

Source: Statistical Abstract for the United Kingdom, Eightieth Number (1937), pp. 374 and 154, 155.

More Recent Conclusions of Economic Historians

No consensus has emerged on the effects of the tariff even as distance from the event has increased. The tariff has never been far from discussion since the Second World War, but conclusions have as often been asserted as demonstrated. Kahn, for example, claims that United Kingdom imports of manufactures from most of Europe and the United States were, inside twelve to eighteen months, reduced by something like 60 per cent 'as a result of the tariff'.[30] Arndt, on the other hand, contends that by stimulating economic activity, and so income, effective demand was raised and imports actually rose.[31] In other words, the former accepts the primary claim for the tariff that the price effect reduced imports, while the latter points to the peculiar conditions of the time (high unemployment and spare capacity), which resulted in growth taking place behind the protective wall. Arthur Lewis states that 'The tariff ... was low and while it was of some assistance, it was not enough to prevent employment from continuing to decline in the protected industries as a whole',[32] thus conflicting with Arndt's implicit belief to the contrary. Hutchinson, the former secretary of the Import Duties Advisory Committee, produced his own account in the 1960s and was, not surprisingly, firmly of the view that the tariff had succeeded in correcting the balance of payments problem.[33]

Pollard agrees with Kahn that there was a reduction of imports but does not attribute it to the tariff. He regards the fall in exports and total foreign trade as being part of a secular trend, 'and may well not have been caused by the tariff as such'.[34]

Richardson is one of few economic historians who have treated the tariff in more depth.[35] While he accepts that the effects of the tariff are better worked out at the sectoral or commodity level and that there are difficulties in isolating the effects of protection, he concludes that 'the effects of the general tariff on imports were not very significant'.[36] This view has entered some textbooks: 'The evidence ... suggests that protection was a somewhat inept weapon' and that there was 'no clear sign that employment recovered first in protected industries'.[37]

More recently there have been some rigorous approaches to estimation of tariff effects for both individual sectors and for the economy as a whole. Foreman-Peck found economies of scale in the car industry and suggests that a tariff would have lowered costs and prices of the British product.[38] Some difficulties were experienced in estimating demand curves but, ignoring these for the moment, the results were that the industry benefited from the tariff and that the benefits of protection for the producer outweighed any loss to the consumer over the years 1920–39 – in other words, this tariff was a net benefit to society. The suggestion is also made that a tariff of similar magnitude could have helped the British industry before 1914. Some of the assumptions of this model are controversial but it remains one of the few attempts to tackle the effects of the tariff in a rigorous fashion.

Foreman-Peck has also produced estimates for effects at a macro level.[39] Emphasising the relative price effects of the tariff – that is, that the tariff diverted expenditure to domestic goods – he argues that the generated multiplier effects increased domestic production significantly. The precise figure attached to this is that Gross Domestic Product was 2.3 per cent higher in 1938 than it would have been in the absence of the tariff. Again, there are several points of debate both for macroeconomists and economic historians, but in another study of similar sophistication similar results have been produced though by a different route. Eichengreen[40] estimates and simulates a general equilibrium model of the British economy designed to identify the impact of the tariff on key macroeconomic variables such as real output, price level and the exchange rate. The results are consistent with the predictions of the theory and are as follows: the tariff was responsible for a dramatic improvement in Britain's terms of trade and for a 20 per cent appreciation of the exchange rate; it brought rises in output, employment and prices and, remarkably, produced exactly the same rise in GDP as Foreman-Peck calculated. Eichengreen stresses, however, that the channels through which the impact was transmitted were quite different in his case. He argues that the tariff improved the terms of trade sufficiently to neutralise the relative price effect of the tariff. The tariff raised output and employment by raising absorption relative to output, inducing a current account deficit and so increasing the equilibrium price level that cleared British financial markets.[41]

One of the interesting conclusions here is that a principal objective of the keenest advocates of the tariff in the interwar years was the elimination of the persistent trade imbalance or, better, current account deficit in the balance of payments. It was claimed by some that this had been achieved, yet the result of Eichengreen's study is to show that just the opposite happened.

Partial Equilibrium Analysis of Impact of Tariff on Imports

This section attempts to provide some indication of the extent of the impact the tariff might have had on the reduction of imports, and by implication the impact on domestic production and employment. This will be done at as great a level of disaggregation as is possible with the data available. The initial procedure has been simply to ignore other variables as we try to isolate the tariff. This is not ideal but it does have certain advantages, one of them being the explicit manner in which it deals with the price elasticities and the nominal tariff, which allows us simply to reach an upper bound on the import-reducing effects of the tariff. Obviously there were interactions between variables that mean that actual figures do not coincide with predicted values, but at least when there are some figures to attach to the strictly tariff effects we are then in a better position to examine what actually happened and to suggest the direction in which these other variables would have operated on the tariff effects. The most important of the other factors, to reiterate, are exchange rates and incomes.

It can be seen from Table 7.4 that there is a variety of estimates of price elasticities for British imports. For total imports there is a range of -0.82 to $+0.23$, though the latter can be set aside on the estimator's own recommendation and we are left with a range of -0.82 to -0.24. In other words, *ceteris paribus*, a 10 per cent tariff should have reduced imports by around 5 per cent.

Most estimates of international trade elasticities have attracted heavy criticism because of their unsatisfactory treatment of methodological problems.[42] Although Brown has been critical of Chang[43] on these grounds, he agrees with him on the general order of magnitude of the estimates made.[44] Chang's method was to run regression equations that were logarithmic functions of the quantity of imports on a home employment index (a surrogate for income), an import price index and in certain cases a domestic price index. At a later date Thackeray tried to improve upon these estimates by substituting real income for the home employment index and by using quarterly data. The results were unsatisfactory, a positive sign being obtained for the price elasticity for total imports, though Thackeray believed the

Table 7.4 Elasticity Estimates and Import Reduction Effects

	Price elasticity of demand for imports		Nominal tariff %	Actual % of reduction over 1930			
	Classes II & III	Class III[1]		Predicted % reduction	1933	1934	1935
Total imports							
Chang -0.28	Class II	Pottery & Glass -5.90	30	177	59	50	48
Niesser -0.24	Chang -0.24	Iron & Steel -1.15	20	23	78	67	68
Thackeray +0.23	Scott -0.20	Non-ferrous Metal -4.50	20	90	55	37	21
		Cutlery/Hardware -1.10	20	22	44	38	33
	Class III	Electrical -5.90	20	118	71	64	63
Friedman -0.82	Chang -1.10	Machinery -2.10	20	42	60	47	38
Moggridge -0.50	Niesser (1924-31) -1.30	Wood & Timber -1.80	20	36	51	47	41
		Cotton Manufactures -4.69	20	94	82	81	80
	Niesser (1932-8) -1.20	Woollen Manufactures -5.40	20	108	86	85	86
		Silk Manufactures -1.12	25	0	72	63	63
	Scott -7.00	Other Textile -1.70	20	34	60	63	63
		Apparel -1.80	20	36	68	62	63
		Vehicles -1.10	31	0	35	12	15

[1] from Chang.

Sources: T. C. Chang, *Cyclical Movements in the Balance of Payments* (1951); H. Niesser and F. Modigliani, *National Incomes and International Trade* (1953); F. G. Thackeray, 'Elasticity of Demand for United Kingdom Imports', *Bulletin of the Oxford University Institute of Statistics* (1950); M. Fg. Scott, *A Study of United Kingdom Imports* (1963); Philip Friedman, *The Impact of Trade Destruction on National Incomes* (1974); D. Moggridge, *The Return to Gold, 1925* (1969).

result to be compatible with a true elasticity of between −0.3 and +0.7 at the 10 per cent probability level.[45]

As we move to the first level of disaggregation we would expect to find some variation in these measures, for we are then looking at Classes where *a priori* differences can be expected. This is borne out for Classes II and III: for Class II (raw materials) it falls slightly to a low of −0.20, and for Class III (manufactures) all estimates are in excess of unity.

However, we are interested in an even greater level of disaggregation, particularly in Class III product groups. Here we expect an increase in the size of the parameters since one commodity group becomes a substitute, however feeble, for another: for example cotton goods for woollen goods or any other textiles or apparel group. Price elasticity estimates at this level of disaggregation are difficult to find. Indeed at the commodity group level for the United Kingdom in the interwar years there are really only Chang's estimates to fall back on. These are shown in Table 7.4. They have a considerable range: from −1.10 for both cutlery and hardware and vehicles to −5.90 for both pottery and glassware and electrical goods. Elasticities of the size of −6.0 clearly have considerable interest over those around unity and the first thing to look at is what these elasticities coupled with their respective nominal tariffs meant in terms of expected reduction in imports. (The assumption being made here is that suppliers left their prices constant.) The range of differences increases now because the highest price elasticity is associated with the highest nominal tariff. Therefore, still proceeding under the *ceteris paribus* assumption, we see that with nominal tariffs (and hence expected price rises) all in the range of 20 per cent to 30 per

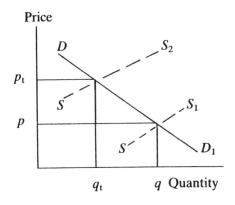

Figure 7.1   Effect of Tariff on Imports

cent, the expected fall in imports ranges from 22 per cent for cutlery and hardware to 177 per cent for pottery and glassware.

Figure 7.1 illustrates what it is that is being measured. Assume that DD_1 represents the demand curve for import X, and that p is the equilibrium price and q the quantity bought. A tariff is added to price, the new price is therefore p_t. The quantity of imports is now reduced to q_t. In the trade returns the values given are the result of pq before the tariff and $p_t q_t$ after the tariff. We wish to capture the reduction in imports, $q - q_t$. We know that the total import prices fell between 1930 and 1933, though the fall was much less for Class III goods than for Classes I and II.[46] The comparison we make then is between pq and pq_t. That is to say the tariff has to be removed from the trade values for the years after 1932. The calculation is therefore:

$$\frac{pq_{1930} - pq_{1933}}{pq_{1930}} \cdot 100$$

Table 7.4 shows the actual percentage change between pq_{1930} and pq_{1933}. 1930 has been selected as the most appropriate year with which to make comparison since it seems the least 'abnormal' year for imports in this period.[47] In fact, no great variation is found when the comparison is made with an average of 1928–31. It could be argued that 1931 would have been a more suitable choice, but this was the worst depression year and world trade continued to be sluggish over the next two or three years. Some duties were imposed in late 1931 and a considerable amount of ordering in anticipation of the tariff was going on in different commodities in 1931, thus lending further distortion to that year.

The question then is, how far do these figures differ from the predicted ones of Table 7.4. We can see that for many of the classes shown in Table 7.4 there is a fairly close correspondence – not necessarily in the size of the figures but in the rankings. For example, cutlery and hardware and wood and timber manufactures are among the lowest predicted reductions and the lowest actual reductions; at the other end of the scale, electrical manufactures and woollen goods are amongst the highest predicted and highest actual values. Against this is iron and steel with a low predicted reduction but rather a large actual reduction. Apparel and other textile goods are in a similar position. This leaves us with rank correlation coefficients of .32 and .30 respectively for 1933 and 1934 – in other words, a poor correspondence between the predicted values and the actual values. So what confidence do these results inspire? The answer must be that they provide a rather poor indication of the effect of the tariff.

When we make a comparison with goods in the same Class where the tariff did not operate our confidence is lessened further. For example, theoretically there should be no further reduction in the vehicles and silk groups, since these had had duties on them for five years prior to 1930 and these duties remained constant at the introduction of the tariff. The reduction in imports of vehicles, particularly for 1934, is very low, but for silk goods it is high. All this would seem to point to the fact that reductions were brought about by some other factor.

Notes

1 *Parliamentary Debates*, 5th Series, Commons, Vol. 261, Cols 287–290.
2 Gerhard Kumleden, *The Workers' Case for Free Trade* (1932), p. 14. This also contained a very clear account of the probable effects of the tariff in Britain.
3 Francis Francis, *The Free Trade Fall* (1926), pp. 28, 29.
4 Quoted by Collin Brooks, *This Tariff Question* (1931), p. 169.
5 A. S. Comyns Carr and D. Rowland Evans, *The Lure of Safeguarding* (1929).
6 Herbert G. Williams, *Through Tariffs to Prosperity* (1931).
7 Lord Arnold, *The Safeguarding of Steel: Fallacies Exposed* (June 1931).
8 Walter Runciman, *The Protection Menace to our Foreign Trade* (November 1930).
9 In Hugh J. Shonfield (ed.), *The Book of British Industries* (1933), p. 71.
10 ibid. p. 207.
11 Cyril Asquith, *The Failure of Protection* (October 1934); Ronald Walker, *Why Tariffs have Failed* (1934); Ronald M. Findlay, *Britain under Protection* (1935).
12 *The Times*, 17 September 1932, No. 741, Vol. XXXI, p. 12.
13 ibid., 30 September 1933, No. 799, Vol. XXXIII, p. 58.
14 *The Economist*, 16 April 1932, pp. 838–9.
15 ibid., 14 May 1932, p. 1069.
16 *Supplement to the Economist*, 18 February 1933.
17 *The Economist*, 13 May p. 1016.
18 H. Leak, 'Some Results of the Import Duties Act', *Journal of the Royal Statistical Society*, part IV (1937).
19 E. V. Francis, *Britain's Economic Strategy* (1939), p. 178.
20 D. R. E. Abel, *A History of British Tariffs, 1923–1942* (1945).
21 F. C. C. Benham, *Great Britain Under Protection* (1941).
22 Political Economic Planning, *Report on International Trade* (1937), p. 73.
23 Public Record Office CAB 27/467, Committee on the Balance of Trade.
24 Public Record Office, T 175/52, *Hopkins Papers*, Letter, 4 March 1931.
25 ibid., Letter, 26 March 1931.
26 ibid.
27 Public Record Office, T 200/2, Macmillan Committee, 1931.
28 Public Record Office, CAB 27/467, BT (31) 11.
29 It may have been wiser to base this ratio on an average of, say, 1928–30, and it is surprising that this was not done.
30 Alfred E. Kahn, *Great Britain in the World Economy* (1946), p. 246.
31 H. W. Arndt, *The Economic Lessons of the Nineteen Thirties* (1944), pp. 102–5.
32 W. A. Lewis, *Economic Survey 1919–1939* (1949), p. 87.
33 Sir Herbert Hutchinson, *Tariff Making and Industrial Reconstruction* (1965).
34 Sidney Pollard, *The Development of the British Economy 1914–1950* (1962), p. 200.

35   H. W. Richardson, *Economic Recovery in Britain, 1932–39* (1967), pp. 236–65. We return to a closer examination of Richardson's results in Chapter 8.

36   ibid., p. 26.

37   L. J. Williams, *Britain and the World Economy 1919–1970* (1971), p. 86.

38   J. Foreman-Peck, 'Tariff Protection and Economies of Scale: The British Motor Industry before 1939', *Oxford Economic Papers* (1979).

39   J. Foreman-Peck, 'The British Tariff and Industrial Protection in the 1930s: An Alternative Model', *Economic History Review* (1981).

40   Barry Eichengreen, 'The British Tariff in the 1930s' (PhD Thesis, 1981).

41   Barry Eichengreen, 'The Macroeconomic Effects of the British General Tariff of 1932', mimeograph (1979).

42   G. H. Orcutt, 'Measurement of Price Elasticities in International Trade', *Review of Economics and Statistics* (1950).

43   T. C. Chang, 'The British Demand for Imports in the Inter-war Period', *Economic Journal* (1946), pp. 188–207.

44   A. J. Brown, 'The Fundamental Elasticities in International Trade', in T. Wilson and W. S. Andrews (eds), *Oxford Studies in the Price Mechanism* (1951), pp. 91–106.

45   F. G. Thackeray, 'Elasticity of Demand for United Kingdom Imports', *Bulletin of the Oxford Institute of Statistics* (1950), pp. 109–14.

46   The index for total imports was as follows: 1930 – 118, 1932 – 89, 1933 – 56, 1934 – 89, 1935 – 80. C. H. Feinstein, *Statistical Tables of National Income, Expenditure and Output of the U.K. 1855–1965* (1976), T.139.

47   This was also the year used by Leak, op.cit. As he points out, 'the volume of retained imports of articles wholly or mainly manufactured … was the same in 1930 as in 1929 and about 5 per cent higher than in 1927 and 1928'. When dutiable goods from other enactments were deducted, the difference between these years was only 2 or 3 per cent.

8

Effective Rates of Protection

Until very recently discussion of the effects of the industrial tariff in the 1930s centred on nominal tariff levels. Where serious attempts at measurement took place they often got bogged down in the dubiousness or clear unreliability of the estimates of elasticities. Sometimes discussion faltered at a point further back, in the unavailability of suitable price and quantity data at a sufficient level of disaggregation to allow useful elasticity estimates to be made. It is therefore clearly desirable to shift attention to an approach that can provide some better indication of the effects of protection, particularly on resource flows in the economy. The approach adopted here is to measure the effective rate of protection. Of course this approach is not adopted simply as a way out of the impasse. Neither should it be thought a simple matter to measure precisely any effects of the tariff. There is an array of difficulties that includes the weakness of the data, the complexity of the tariff structure and the contemporaneous realignment of major world currencies. One problem has been the separation of the many factors at work, but even though this is difficult, and even insoluble, it may nevertheless be possible to point towards the direction of the resource allocation effects of the tariff, particularly for important sectors, and to attach tentative magnitudes to these, rather than rest content with some of the assertions of the past, of the kind: 'There can be no doubt that the Act of 1932 helped immediately. It provided revenue, reduced the pressure of imports, improved the balance of payments.'[1]

A brief outline of the theory of effective protection is provided here together with estimates of effective protection in Britain in the 1930s, which are compared with the results of the more conventional approach.

The Theory of Effective Protection

Effective protection is a relatively recent addition to international trade theory. It gives expression to the margin of protection on value-added in the production process rather than simply that on the product price. It is thus of crucial importance to the producer. A tariff on an import for which there is a domestic substitute gives protection to the domestic producer. But if a tariff is placed on an import that is an input in domestic industry then the user of that input is taxed. If he is the same user he is being both protected and taxed and it is desirable to ascertain the net effect on the value-added. That does not seem very difficult and of course businessmen, tariff-making authorities and even economists have been well aware that a tariff on an input is a tax on the final product. But calculations of tariffs and tariff effects were almost always in terms of nominal rates. It was not until the 1960s that the idea was incorporated into international trade literature.[2]

The following example illustrates the calculation of the effective rate:[3] product A has an import price of £1.00 while the cost of its material inputs on the world market is 60p, leaving a value-added of 40p. A 20 per cent tariff on product A raises its domestic price to £1.20 while a 10 per cent tariff on the material inputs raises costs to the domestic producer to 66p. Protection enables firms to operate with a value-added of 54p (the difference between the domestic price and the material input) as against 40p abroad. This margin of 14p means the effective rate of protection on the domestic processing activity is 35 per cent – the percentage difference between the 'old' value-added and the 'new' value-added.

Thus the measurement of effective protection requires estimation of the following equation:

$$g_j = \frac{t_j - \sum\limits_{(i=1)}^{n} a_{ij} - t_i}{1 - \sum\limits_{(i=1)}^{n} a_{ij}}$$

where g_j = the symbol adopted for effective protection
        t_j = nominal tariff on the output
        t_i = nominal tariff on the input
        a_{ij} = coefficient of intermediate inputs per unit of output j.

Some implications of this can be stated briefly here. First, the nominal and effective rates of protection will differ only if the tariff rate imposed on the finished product differs from that on the intermediate product. Where $t_j > t_i$, then $g_j > t_j > t_i$; if $t_j < t_i$ then $g_j < t_i$; and if $t_j < a_{ij}t_i$, then $g_j < 0$. It should be noted that g_j can be negative even though the nominal rate is positive. Following from this, if there is no nominal tariff on the final product but there is one on an intermediate product, the effective protective rate must be negative. All of these implications hold when there are varying tariff rates on different inputs. Also, for any given nominal tariff rate, the smaller the value-added of a process the greater the effective rate. Johnson suggests that 'value added typically runs somewhat under one half of sales value', and that 'effective protection rates on manufactures are typically one and a half times to twice as high as the nominal tariff rates, and they rise progressively with the stage of production or degree of fabrication of the product'.[4]

One of the concerns of the Import Duties Advisory Committee in the 1930s, as we noted earlier, was to keep duty on raw materials low (they were zero initially and in many cases stayed there). This points to the distinct possibility that the effective rate of protection may have been quite high in the 1930s, even though nominal rates often appeared moderate or even low.

A further reason for effective rates being of interest (over and above being able to say that industry X had a greater degree of protection than industry Y, in spite of an identical or lower nominal tariff) is that they shed light on the direction of resource allocation effects of the tariff structure. In the words of Corden:

> If we have calculated that tradable industry X has 10 per cent effective protection and tradable industry Y has 20 per cent we should be able to conclude that resources will be drawn from X into Y and into both from non-protected tradable industries and from those non-traded industries where prices have stayed constant.[5]

Estimates of Effective Protection in Britain in the 1930s

The object of this investigation is to look at as much of the industrial sector as data permit, and to show the extent of protection afforded individual industries according to the concept of the effective protection rate. Chapter 3 outlined the development of protectionist legislation and showed that, although policy changes had taken place before 1931, the volume of imports affected was nevertheless very small. When the general tariff was introduced in April 1932 the position changed. From April 1932 onwards the Import Duties Advisory Committee considered applications for increased tariffs and made many recommendations for implementation by the president of the Board of Trade.[6] But many of the recommendations were of a trifling nature as far as the tariff as a whole was concerned and for our purposes can be largely ignored. The main features of the tariff were: (a) most imports of raw materials and most imports from the Empire were free; (b) almost all other imports were subject to duty. Furthermore, most rates of duty were fairly moderate. Many manufactures had rates of 10 or 20 per cent on them, but rates above this level were relatively rare. The net result was something like this: 25 per cent of all imports came in free of duty (though some of these were restricted in other ways); 50 per cent paid nominal rates of 10–20 per cent; 8 per cent paid nominal rates of more than 20 per cent; the remaining 17 per cent of imports were paying either the old McKenna duties or safeguarding duties.[7]

Problems of Measurement and Analysis

The range of this investigation is, as is frequently the case, shaped in part by the availability or accessibility of certain data. In this exercise the value-added in the production process is required together with input coefficients. There are very few studies of such a kind and they have much more limited information than modern input–output tables. Material for some industries was available from a study by Barna for 1935.[8] Barna's table is restricted to thirty-six industries in all, which of course is less than ideal and not surprisingly has the further limitation of having industries grouped in a way that does not correspond exactly with the industries as given in the *Customs and Excise Tariff*. For example, Barna groups cotton and silk goods together while the tariff separates them, with silk belonging to the 'key industry' duties group. It is therefore not possible to obtain a reliable figure for value-added in cotton or silk production from Barna's study and therefore not possible to calculate the effective protection rate, unless we employ certain assumptions about the proportion of value-added. For this reason, the information available in Barna was supplemented with material from the 1935 and 1948 censuses of production. In some cases the two groupings are not identical but are close enough to allow a calculation that while not of a high degree of precision nevertheless is useful for our purposes. In all the examples presented, a figure for the effective protection rate is provided but these figures should not be regarded as final – rather as guides to the order of magnitude of protection afforded.

There are some further points that require clarification. In using an 'input–output' table for 1935 (that is, three years after the imposition of the general tariff), there may be an incorporation of the effects of protection while the basic formula for estimation has been conceived in terms of free trade value-added. This problem has been tackled in several ways in empirical studies. The first has been in effect to ignore it by making the assumption of fixed technology – that the tariff will not affect input coefficients in the short run.[9] Another approach has been to take a country with few or very low nominal tariffs and to use this as a proxy for the free trade technology in other countries. For example, in Belassa's study of industrialised countries he took the Netherlands, which had a very low tariff, as a surrogate for the free trade technology and used their input coefficients and value-added for all other countries.[10] A third corrective procedure has been to use the domestic input–output relationships observed in the protected country and to infer the free market coefficient by assuming that free trade prices are equal to protected prices deflated by the appropriate tariff-rates.[11] Thus, for the formula given above,

$$a_{ij} = \frac{p'_{i,j}/(1 + t_i)}{p'_{j}/(1 + t_j)} \, ,$$

where $p'_{i,j}$ and p'_{j} are the values of input i per unit of output and the unit value of output of industry j respectively.

Each of these procedures has its own deficiencies. The last mentioned has the difficulties of price selection and data availability. The second is clearly not possible for a study of the 1930s where almost all comparable industrial countries had imposed high nominal tariffs; even if there were such a low-tariff or free trade industrial country, the possibility of there being an input–output table available for it that would even resemble the one we have to work from is remote. The first approach is an easy solution, which does not alter the fact that it may be the most satisfying on theoretical grounds. Three years is a relatively short period and no industry shows marked changes in input coefficients when a comparison is made between the 1930 and 1935 *Census of Production*. Therefore the first approach is the one used here.

One point that makes the investigation easier in some respects than a similar modern inquiry is that there is little problem with the summation of inputs at varying nominal tariff rates, since, as mentioned before, tariffs on inputs were few and where they did occur they tended to be at one rate only. Value-added is equal to 1 minus the inputs.

It is appropriate, finally, to mention the exchange rate. Britain left the gold standard in September 1931 and let the pound drift downwards for some months until it was around 30 per cent lower in relation to the gold currencies. The exchange rate was then stabilised and manipulated via the Exchange Equalisation Account. Thus British trade may be thought to have been given assistance by a depreciating currency at roughly the same time as the tariff was imposed and one of the difficulties confronting those attempting to say anything about the effect of this tariff has been to separate the price

Table 8.1 *Nominal Tariffs and Effective Rates of Protection*

	(1) Gross output (£m.)	(2) Nominal tariff	Pref.	(3) % Value-added I	(4) % Value-added II	Effective rate of protection Rank[1]	I	Effective rate of protection II
1 Building	345.8	0		53.2	58	33	−7.2	−10.8
2 Iron & Steel Manufacturing	192.4	20		37.7	51	31	16.7	7.8
3 Motor Vehicles	129.5	33⅓	22⅔%	39.8	53	12	53.5 (25.6)³	50 (weighted for pref.)
4 Electrical Engineering	106.8	20		53.7		24	37.3	
5 Timber Trades²	78.7	20		47.4	52	17	42.2	38.4
6 Cotton Spinning & Doubling	74.3	20		27.2	37	3	73.5	54.0
7 Cotton Weaving	69.4	20		29.5		5	67.8	
8 Chemicals	68.8	33⅓		53.2	52	8	62.7	63.4
9 Worsted	64.4	20		32.1		9	62.3	
10 Non-ferrous Metals	54.6	20		30.8	34	6	65.0	
11 Shipbuilding	45.8	0		49.8		32	−6.1	58.8
12 Woollen	44.5	20		44.9	43	16	44.5	46.5
13 Boot & Shoe	42.0	20		47.8		18	41.8	
14 Furniture	39.5	20		51.4		23	38.9	
15 Silk	36.1	—		39.1				
16 Rubber	28.1	20		50.9		22	39.3	
17 Soap, Candles, Perfumery	26.3	20		50.2		21	39.8	
18 Tramways & Light Railways	24.4	33⅓		57.8	57	26=	33.3	53.8
19 Paint, Colour & Varnish	22.2	20		49.1		19	40.7	
20 Railway Carriage & Wagon	17.9	33⅓		61.4	57	26=	33.3	53.8
21 Glass	17.2	—		17.2	65			

No.	Item							
22	Building Materials	15.9	20/30		53.5		14	46.7	
23	China & Earthenware	14.2	30		66.2		15	45.3	
24	Hat & Cap	10.7	30	48	46.7		7=	64.2	41.6
25	Lace	7.2	30		38.9		2	77.1	
26	Fur	5.5	30		41.2		4	72.8	
27	Glove	3.0	30	48	46.7		7=	64.2	41.6
28	Manufacturing Abrasives								
29	Roofing Felt	1.3	15		46.2		27	32.5	
30	Umbrella	1.1	20		36.4		10	54.9	
15a	Silk: articles where: Silk>20%	36.1 {	36.1	43	39.1 {		20	39.9(22.2)[3]	54(40)[3]
b	5% < Silk < 20%		16.6	20			28	28.2(14.4)[3]	
c	Silk < 5%		10.0	12			30	25.0(19.9)[3]	
21a	Glass: Plate & Sheet	17.2 {	15/20		61.6 {	65	29	28.0	23.2
b	Domestic		30				13	48.4	30.2
c	Optical		50				1	80.7	} 76.9
d	Scientific		33⅓				11	53.8	

[1] Indicates the ranking according to the effective rate of protection.

[2] Includes furniture (No. 14), which is also given separately.

[3] The figures in brackets give the rate using the preferential nominal tariff. In the case of silk, specific duties were converted to *ad valorem* using price data from *The Economist*, 22 June 1935, p. 1467.

Sources: (1) *Fifth Census of Production and the Import Duties Act Inquiry, 1935*, Parts I, II, III and IV, and *Census of Production, 1948*, Vols 3 and 4.
(2) *Customs and Excise Tariff of the United Kingdom of Great Britain and Northern Ireland* (1935).
(3) Calculated from *Census of Production*, 1935 and 1948.
(4) T. Barna, 'The Interdependence of the British Economy, *JRSS*, Part I (1952), pp. 29–77.

effects of the tariff from those of the falling exchange rate. However, to some extent that difficulty is avoided here, since the principal concern is the effect of the tariff on resource flows. In any case, within the conventional framework of tariff analysis, many countries either immediately realigned their currencies with the UK or their abandonment of gold during 1929–31 left their currency in a close relationship to sterling by 1932.[12] As the bulk of British trade was with countries whose currencies moved with hers, there was probably little significant exclusion of imports into the UK or indeed rise in exports from the UK as a result of the devaluation of sterling.[13] If currencies were in the main not out of alignment, then the change in imports must have had some other cause.

Results and Implications

Having discussed the problems of measurement and analysis it remains to present the results and discuss some implications. Table 8.1 presents the nominal tariffs and effective rates of protection for thirty selected industries and some sub-groups for silk and glass, (ERPI) together with effective rates for the smaller number of industries covered by Barna (ERP II). These rates are based on two sets of figures for value-added. One is calculated from *Census of Production*, 1935 and 1948; the other is taken from Barna. The first point to make about the results in general is that the effective rate of protection is typically not far removed from twice the size of the nominal rate. This is in agreement with other empirical studies and of course derives essentially from the fact that value-added in the production process is in the vicinity of 50 per cent of the sales value.

Where preferential tariff rates operated, an effective rate of protection has been calculated allowing for this in the nominal rate. In the case of silk they can be safely ignored, for only infinitesimal quantities of silk goods came from Empire producers – in 1929, of a total value of manufactured silk imported of £13.2m., only £0.06m. (0.4 per cent) came from the Empire and enjoyed preferential duties.[14] In the motor vehicles sector, however, the preference cannot be ignored because one Empire producer, Canada, was relatively important. Both rates have therefore been computed and a weighted average calculated. In 1929 the preferential duty collected was £121,215, while the duty on foreign cars was £594,507.[15] This ratio of .202 is not very different for any of the previous four years (when of course there was a tariff on this sector) and so it was used as the basis for the weighted average. The weighted average nominal rate produces an effective rate that does not, however, differ much from the original value. A further point that should be made is that in the case of motor vehicles, where the tariff had been in operation almost uninterrupted since the First World War, we do not weaken our assumption of 'fixed technology', for the tariff on inputs did not fall until 1932.

There is a moderately close association between nominal rates and effective rates. The Spearman's rank correlation coefficient for all industries is .473, while that for the smaller number of industries is .521. These are lower than other studies have found but in line with the suggestion that the association between nominal and effective rates becomes closer as tariff structures have become more sophisticated.[16] There are, however, (as in some other studies), some notable exceptions to this pattern where the effective rate is less than the nominal rate and two cases where it is negative.[17] We shall look at these cases first.

The building industry[18] is of interest for a number of reasons, not least because much attention has been given to it by virtue of its size and because of its supposed role in the recovery of the economy from the depression. Both Benham, writing some few years after the depression, and more recently Richardson have credited the building industry with the crucial contribution to the upturn in 1932/3. The reasons behind the expansion of building were a combination of demand factors such as growing population of house-buying age, and rising real incomes (resulting from falling prices and steady money wages) with an institutional factor – namely, the availability of finance from the building societies at modest rates of interest. What is of particular interest here is that the result suggests that the industry had a negative effective rate of protection;[19] that is, the industry was taxed in some way. The negative rate is arrived at by observing that the final product, housing, cannot be protected by tariffs, whereas the *importable* inputs, which constituted 42 per cent of the final product, had tariffs on them. The inputs included bricks, roofing tiles and slates, glass, builders' woodwork, metal door and window frames and so on, and the tariffs levied on these items ranged from 15 per cent to 33⅓ per cent. It is not possible to state accurately what percentage each of these inputs comprised and it is not possible therefore to use the equation to its best advantage. The calculation that suggests the sector had a negative rate of protection of 7.2 per cent is based on a nominal tariff of 20 per cent on half the inputs and a zero rate on the other half, which is close to a minimum rate. The upper bound can be found by using the 33⅓ per cent nominal rate on all inputs, which produces a negative effective rate of 24.1 per cent. The true rate lies between these two points, and the judgement is that it is closer to the former than to the latter. As mentioned before, great precision cannot be achieved and the object is simply to establish that the industry was disadvantaged to some relatively severe extent.

If we accept that the growing demand for housing and its gradual satisfaction was important for economic recovery, but concede that the industry was handicapped by higher costs because of the tariff,[20] then it is necessary to pay even greater tribute to this sector for its role in recovery. There is a minor complication here, in that it was the declared policy of the National Government in the midst of economic depression to raise prices and thus boost business confidence, raise investment and so on. If the tariff did raise prices, then it did play a part in stimulating growth. Nevertheless the tariff could be used in other areas to achieve this goal and it can be claimed that such a result as the one obtained here (if accepted) was a second-best solution for the industry and the economy.

The other industry with a negative rate of effective protection is shipbuilding. This industry suffered from a tax on inputs while there was no tariff on the final product.

The result for the iron and steel industry was an effective rate of protection lower than the nominal rate. This is of particular interest because, like building, this was a very large sector that reputedly also gave great stimulus to recovery.[21] The fact that iron and steel can pass through so many stages before it reaches its final form makes it difficult to define the industry. Very simply, it can be divided into two parts: the 'heavy' part, producing pig iron, semi-finished products and the simpler rolled products; and the 'light' part, where re-rolling and finishing is carried out along with the production of more special-ised goods. Some firms covered most processes, but it was mainly those engaged in the heavy part who sought the tariff. The 'heavy' part was the predominant part of the industry in every way and on this issue they were triumphant. The tariff levied on 'finished' goods was 20 per cent, while that on raw materials (which ranged from ingots, sheet and tinplate bars to forgings and castings) was 33⅓ per cent. Clearly the light part resisted a tariff on what were their inputs, though at the same time they were given protection on finished goods.

There is a marked discrepancy between Barna's value-added (II) and my value-added (I) for this industry, which arises out of this difficulty of definition. If we accept Barna's value-added for the iron and steel industry as a whole at 51 per cent we get an effective rate of protection of 7.8 per cent. Although to disaggregate would be to do some violence to the definition of the industry, if we treated the two parts of the industry separately then the heavy part would have a positive rate of effective protection while the lighter part would have a negative rate. On the basis of the calculation using separately estimated value-added, the overall effective rate would still, at 16.7 per cent, be lower than the nominal rate, but not by much. In other words, this is another case where the industry appeared to be afford-ed considerable protection but in fact the protection given to value-added in production was relatively small – least of all by a long way in the manufacturing sector. Yet this is the industry credited with making the greatest contribution to recovery in that sector. Of course it may indeed have made an important contribution to recovery, but if so then we should have to look elsewhere for the reasons, for the tariff does not appear to have been an important one.

There are some further interesting points in the results. When the industries are ranked according to the degree of effective protection afforded, despite the moderately close association mentioned earlier, there are some industries where tariff protection was thought to be high at the time but where by this measure it is seen to be low, and vice versa. Some parts of the silk industry, for example, had the second highest nominal rate and other parts were also high, but they lie well down in the bottom half of the list when ranked by the effective rate. The major parts of the cotton industry, on the other hand, had the most common (20 per cent) nominal tariff but are in the top five as measured by effective protection.

If we revert to the allocation of resources theme, the results would lead us to suggest resources should have been drawn towards certain branches of glass manufacturing, possibly chemicals, the old staples cotton and woollen goods together with clothing (hat and cap, glove, fur, umbrella and so on) and motor vehicles. These at any rate are some of the industries lying in the top half of the rankings. At the other end of the scale are some of the 'new' industries – electrical goods, some types of glass – together with those old staples iron and steel and shipbuilding. Is there any evidence that resources were drawn away from the least protected towards the most protected sectors? It would be reckless to answer this with any haste. If investment funds were taken as a resource and found flowing in a direction at variance with what is suggested from these results it may have been because advantages elsewhere outweighed the benefits of a higher effective rate. Or it may be that the peak of an investment cycle appears in some sector.

In the iron and steel industry, for example, investment in fact rose, and Benham claims that this was because the high level of protection (read from nominal rates) raised confidence. But, given the low rate of effective protection in this industry, we should look for other causes – for example, rationalisation or cartel arrangements. The rationalisation of the industry was linked with the tariff, since the tariff was given and sustained as part of a bargain made between the industry and government in exchange for promises to rationalise, which did not come to fruition until the late 1930s. How effective the cartel arrangements were in limiting imports and promoting domestic goods is difficult to assess but certainly many of those writing on the industry have written in terms of the tariff providing protection rather than the cartels. For example Burn says, 'The imposition of the tariff... had the immediate effect of giving the British makers a greater proportion of the home market for finished and semi-finished steel...'.[22] Minchinton claims that the tariff on imported steel '...stopped the imports of foreign tinplate bars and therefore indirectly influenced the price of domestic bars'.[23] Others have been more reticent, making little claim either way.

Similar difficulties arise with employment. It may not be clear whether or not a tendency was already under way to move to or from a more capital-intensive technique or whether improved employment was for exogenous reasons, such as the independent growth of a market or the decline of a competitor elsewhere. Some hint of the degree of association can be obtained from the Spearman rank correlation coefficient of productivity and effective rates on a limited number of (ten) sectors. The degree of aggregation will have distorted the result somewhat, as will the fact that the productivity increase was that over the period 1924–35. Nevertheless, the correlation coefficient of .503 does suggest some degree of relationship.

It may be worth stressing the point that, although the measure of effective protection suggests that resources will flow from industries with relatively low rates of effective protection and to industries with high rates, there is no guarantee that such a thing happened. Prospective profits could have been high enough to attract extra capital and labour: so long as the labour force is growing or underemployed and/or so long as net investment is positive, resources can flow into one industry without being drawn from another. Equally, high effective rates may be found in stagnant industries if prospects are bad and confidence low.

A final point is that some industries enjoyed other forms of protection and for this reason resources flowed to them and not to others. It is nevertheless worth reiterating that the effective rate simply suggests how responsible the tariff should have been in this area. Unfortunately there are very few studies of twentieth-century industries that touch on these problems. Those that do tend to accept that the tariff was useful. For example, on the glass industry Barker says,

> Very soon the new sheet glass process was turning loss into profit; and the return to protection strengthened Pilkington's position still further. Sheet and glass became subject to an *ad valorem* import duty of 10 per cent and shortly afterwards this 10 per cent duty was raised to 15 per cent. The tariff encouraged Sheet Glass Ltd., to restart their Fourcault machines at Queenborough...[24]

We can return now to a brief comparison of the results of this chapter with those of Richardson, his being one of the few serious attempts in the 1930s to assess the impact of the tariff.[25] Richardson employs what he calls an import replacement ratio in order to measure the effect of protection. The ratio is defined as the rise in gross output, less the rise in exports, over the fall in imports. This was designed to capture the relationship between an industry's expansion of production for the home market and the fall in imports of that industry's products. Employing the *ceteris paribus* assumption and assuming a constant level of domestic demand, the import duty should divert to home production an amount equivalent to the drop in imports. The theoretical norm should be 1.[26] Richardson's results provide examples such as the following. In the electrical goods industry the ratio is 6; in other words, a tariff that reduced imports by 10 per cent increased domestic output (less exports) by 60 per cent. By the same method we find that the tariff would increase pig iron production by 273 per cent. It should be pointed out that, although there would appear to be the difficulty of *post hoc ergo propter hoc* (i.e. simply observing changes after the tariff and attributing them to the tariff), Richardson carries out the same exercise for industries unaffected by the tariff and the lack of significant difference between the two leads him to conclude: 'When the situation between 1930 and 1935 is compared, the surprising conclusion is that the fall in imports in newly protected industries was *less* than the fall in imports of other industries.'[27]

The rank correlation coefficient between our measure of effective protection and Richardson's is −.333, which simply brings out the lack of a relationship between the two measures. This exercise has severe limitations, however, since only ten of the thirty-four industries were closely comparable.

Now it can of course be argued that no approach thus far has satisfactorily separated and identified the effects of the various forces at work, but at least the concept of the effective rate of protection provides an avenue hitherto unexplored for the examination of the tariff in this period. This chapter has argued that, in spite of the limitations mentioned we can obtain a clearer idea of which industries should have been placed in the most, and which in the least, advantageous positions as a result of the tariff, although the use made of protection by an individual industry would have depended on a number of factors.

There are two final cautions. One has been made many times before: the implicit assumption of infinite supply elasticity from the rest of the world leads to an overestimation of the effective protection rates, which should therefore be adjusted downwards. To carry out any quantitative adjustment to the results, however, would simply lend a spurious sense of accuracy to what can only be guides to degrees of protection.

The other point, which has not been given so much attention in

Table 8.2 *Proportion of Output Exported in Selected Industries, 1935*

Industry	% exported
Cotton and silk	41
Woollen and worsted	33
Non-ferrous metals	25
Shipbuilding	23
Chemicals	22
Iron and steel manufacturing	18
Rubber	17
Electrical engineering	14
China and earthenware	13
Motor vehicles	12
Lace	11
Soap, candle, perfumery	10
Building materials	4
Timber trades	1

Source: calculated from *Annual Statement of Trade of the United Kingdom* and *Fifth Census of Production and Import Duties Act Inquiry (1935)*.

the literature, is this: if a protected industry exports, then the part of its output that is exported will not benefit from the tariff since it is sold on the world market. If total output is exported a tariff is useless and the effective rate would be ignored; it follows that the higher the percentage of output exported by any one industry, the less is that industry able to exploit domestic protection. Table 8.2 gives an indication of the level of exports from a number of industries. In cotton and silk and in woollen and worsted, over one-third of output was exported, and in three other industries – non-ferrous metals, shipbuilding and chemicals – something between one-quarter and one-fifth was the proportion sold abroad. In all other cases the proportion was less than one-fifth. What this means is that for cotton and silk the effective rate of protection is only of use and meaning for 60 per cent of output, for woollen and worsted 67 per cent, and so on. Thus care should be taken to give less weight to an industry that exports a large part of its output. Having said that, it should also be noted that most industries are not greatly affected by this point, though again some mental adjustment might be carried out if only to suggest a slightly modified reordering of the rankings.

Notes

1 H. Hutchinson, *Tariff Making and Industrial Reconstruction* (1965), p. 161.

2 See W. M. Corden, *The Theory of Protection* (1971), pp. 245–9. The theory has
  been developed chiefly by Johnson, Balassa, Basevi and Corden and empirical
  investigations have been made by Bela Balassa, 'Tariff Protection in Industrial
  Countries: 'An Evaluation', *Journal of Political Economy* (1965), and Georgio
  Basevi, 'The United States Tariff Structure: Estimates of Effective Rates of
  Protection of United States Industries and Industrial Labour', *Review of Economic and Statistics* (1966), amongst others. Very few attempts have been made by
  economic historians, but one example is found in V. Sundararajan, 'The Impact of
  the Tariff on Some Selected Products of the U.S. Iron and Steel Industry
  1870–1914', *Quarterly Journal of Economics* (1970), pp. 590–610, and another is
  G. R. Hawke, 'The United States Tariff and Industrial Protection in the Late
  Nineteenth Century', *Economic History Review* (1975), pp. 84–99.
3 Adapted from Bela Balassa *et al.*, *The Structure of Protection in Developing
  Countries*.
4 H. G. Johnson, 'Trade Preferences and Developing Countries', *Lloyds Bank
  Review* (1966), pp. 16 and 15.
5 W. M. Corden, 'The Structure of a Tariff System and the Effective Protective
  Rate', *Journal of Political Economy*, (1966), p. 227.
6 See Hutchinson, op.cit., for a discussion of the workings of this Committee and a
  record of how the tariff changed from time to time.
7 The source for the tariff is the *Customs and Excise Tariff of the United Kingdom of
  Great Britain and Northern Ireland* (1935). A useful summary of protective
  measures is given in J. Henry Richardson, 'Tariffs, Preferences and Other Forms
  of Protection', in British Association, *Britain in Recovery* (1938). A more extensive account of the development of the tariff can be found in D. Abel, *A History of
  British Tariffs, 1923–1942* (1945), and in F. C. C. Benham, *Great Britain under
  Protection* (1941). A detailed picture is presented in E. B. McGuire, *The British
  Tariff System* (1951).
8 T. Barna, 'The Interdependence of the British Economy', *Journal of the Royal
  Statistical Society* (1952), pp. 29–77.
9 See Bela Balassa, 'Tariff Protection in Industrial Countries', op.cit., p. 578. See
  also H. G. Grubel and H. Johnson, *Effective Tariff Protection* (1971).
10 Balassa, ibid.
11 T. S. Barker and S. S. Han, 'Effective Rates of Protection for United Kingdom
   Production', *Economic Journal* (1971), pp. 282–93.
12 The depreciation of sterling was followed almost immediately by Canada, India,
   Iceland, Denmark, Egypt, Norway and Sweden leaving the gold standard. This
   meant that between 1929 and 1932 the total number of countries that had depreciated in relation to gold was thirty-two.
13 It should be remembered that, along with the speculative movement of funds, by
   1933 the United States had devalued and that by 1934 most of the important
   currencies were back in alignment.
14 *Annual Statement of Trade of the United Kingdom 1929* (1930), Vol. I, pp. 2, 3.
   1929 is not an unreasonable year to select as a guide here, since duties on silk were
   in force then under the Safeguarding of Industries Act.
15 ibid., Vol. III.
16 Barker and Han, op.cit., p. 292, had a correlation coefficient of .9 for the UK for
   1963 while Hawke, op.cit., p. 92, had a coefficient of between .6 and .7 for the
   United States for 1899 and 1904.
17 Balassa too found various examples of negative rates in different countries; see
   'Tariff Protection in Industrial Countries', op.cit., p. 580, he also found that ships
   in the UK had a negative effective rate. Barker and Han, op.cit., have other
   examples.
18 This is defined by Barna, op.cit., p. 65, as: building and contracting, local
   authorities' works, railway company construction, tramway and light railway

company construction, canal, dock and harbour companies, and certain government departments works.

19   By certain criteria it can be argued that we have a meaningless result here since the final product is not a traded good. But the purpose is to show that taxed inputs leave a sector worse off than before.

20   One possible retort to this line of argument is that price was not a major factor; the important element in house purchase was availability of finance.

21   Most notably, Benham, op.cit.

22   D. L. Burn, *The Economic History of Steelmaking 1867–1939* (1940), p. 450.

23   W. E. Minchinton, *The British Tinplate Industry* (1957), p. 162.

24   T. C. Barker, *Pilkington Brothers and the Glass Industry* (1960), p. 207.

25   Richardson, op.cit., pp. 236–48.

26   ibid., p. 248.

27   ibid., p. 246.

9

Other Considerations

No consideration of the effects of the tariff would be complete without at least some mention of three other interrelated factors of commercial policy. First, in view of the Chancellor's statement that the tariff would improve Britain's bargaining strength in trade negotiations, it is worth looking at the trade agreements concluded soon after the introduction of the tariff, and indicating something of the significance these had in British commercial policy in the 1930s. The second factor that requires some mention is the exchange rate, for the abandonment of the gold standard in September 1931 and the subsequent fall in the value of sterling produced some effect on trade variables similar in direction to that of the tariff. Finally some brief discussion is given of the effects of imperial preference. As we have seen in Chapter 8, this had little impact on industrial protection but it did nevertheless affect longer-term trading relations by virtue of the ill-feeling that it generated in important trading partners such as the United States.

Trade Negotiations

Bilateral trade agreements were a new feature in British policy in the 1930s. Prior to the introduction of the general tariff, some idea of the likely reception of the measure was sought by government from its trade missions abroad.[1] It became clear from the questionnaires returned that a general tariff of 10 per cent *ad valorem* was not going to provoke any grave deterioration in relations with foreign states; in fact, in many parts of Europe the size of the proposed tariff was greeted with relief. After the shock of the abandonment of gold in September, and the loud protests against the Abnormal Import Duties Act of November and its accompaniment the Horticultural Products Act, the general tariff legislation seemed to cause no great consternation. The following list provides a summary of a cross-section of European response to the proposed tariff:[2]

Austria	'resignation'
Czechoslovakia	'public opinion rudely shaken'
Switzerland	'less interested in buying British goods'
Belgium	'severe blow, setback to enlightened opinion'
Netherlands	'resentment'
Italy	'dismay – 19 per cent of Italian exports affected'
Germany	'consternation – demands for retaliation'

Clearly the concern expressed was not too serious, though there was always the threat in the background that the tariff could be hoisted high against any particularly difficult or uncooperative trading partner and this may have contributed to the desire on the part of some to negotiate.[3]

In July 1932 preparations began to be made for these tariff negotiations. Table 9.1 lists the agreements made and the principal commercial notes exchanged, in chronological order. Fifteen countries signed some form of commercial agreement with Britain (over and above the various bilateral agreements signed with Empire countries in Ottawa in August 1932) in the two years from mid-1933 to mid-1935. The great majority were Scandinavian or Baltic. The agreement with Argentina allowed for specific arrangements on meat, but was partly a measure for debt collection.[4] Not too much should be made of these trade agreements as far as British imports and the industrial tariff are concerned, although they had some significance for the import of food and raw materials. They had more significance for some British exports (for example, coal), and for negotiating some minor tariff concessions in other countries on textiles and machinery.

The negotiations with most countries were usually lengthy and complicated but the subjects of discussion often meant little for trade magnitudes or the overall trading pattern. In the agreement with Sweden (which tended to set the pattern for all the other Scandinavian and Baltic countries), the most important concessions made by Britain were on iron and steel products made from charcoal. For British exports to Sweden, where the tariff was in any case low, the objective was to 'conventionalise' existing arrangements. Some of these negotiations reached pitifully low levels and might magnanimously be regarded as an exercise in job creation at a period of serious unemployment. There were long deliberations on items of trifling import. For example, at the first meeting of the Anglo-Swedish negotiations in December 1932 the Swedish delegation inquired 'whether a reduction on confectionery, confined to confectionery not containing chocolate, would be of importance to the United Kingdom?'[5] On 17 December the delegation represented that 'whereas Sweden imports United Kingdom tennis and golf balls, they

Table 9.1   *Trade Agreements with Britain, 1932–5*

Agreement with	Date
1 Denmark	November 1932
2 Germany (exchange of notes)	April 1933
3 Argentina	May 1933
4 Norway	May 1933
5 Sweden	May 1933
6 Iceland	May 1933
7 Finland	September 1933
8 Russia	February 1934
9 France	June 1934
10 Estonia	July 1934
11 Lithuania	July 1934
12 Poland	February 1935
13 Italy	April 1935
14 Turkey	June 1935
15 Uruguay	June 1935
16 South Africa	August 1935

Source: The agreements can be found in *British Parliamentary Papers* as follows: (1) Cmd 4298; (2) Cmd 4297; (3) Cmd 4310, 4492; (4) Cmd 4324, 4500; (5) Cmd 4324; (6) Cmd 4331; (7) Cmd 4425, 4472; (8) Cmd 4513; (9) 4590, 4632; (10) Cmd 4653; (11) Cmd 4648; (12) Cmd 4820; (13) Cmd 4883, 4888; (14) Cmd 4925; (15) Cmd 4940; (16) Cmd 5012.

export to the United Kingdom all other descriptions of rubber balls. They come into the United Kingdom under, "Rubber balls, other descriptions"'. The value of this item was about £3,000 and a reduction of duty from 25 per cent to 20 per cent *ad valorem* was being sought – in other words, a potential saving of £150 in the middle of the greatest collapse in world trade for generations. After careful consideration the British negotiators were able to return three months later with the answer 'no'![6]

In the case of France an exchange of notes took place in 1933.[7] The reason for this was that the Convention of Commerce and Navigation signed at Paris in 1882 was due to terminate in May 1934 and to avoid any difficulties before a new treaty was signed it was proposed that the conventions be continued. In June 1934 a new agreement was signed employing the most-favoured-nation principle and including some minor specific quotas. There was also an exchange of notes with Germany in 1933, the essence of which was that certain German products (some chemicals, musical instruments, clocks) would be granted minor tariff concessions in Britain in exchange for a quantity of licences for the import into Germany of 180,000 metric tons per month of British coal and coke.

The agreement signed with South Africa was a somewhat different affair. Britain simply wanted to hold on to preferences already established when South Africa introduced its new Customs Act that year.

The claim has sometimes been made that concessions secured by Britain were obtained more easily where the foreign country ran a favourable trade balance with Britain, because the country concerned could be asked to bring about a greater equality of trade by increasing its imports from Britain.[8] Government too was of this view, believing that a country with a favourable trade balance with the United Kingdom found it more difficult to retaliate. All European countries, except a handful on the geographical fringe, had favourable trade balances with Britain,[9] but there is little evidence to suggest that they fared any differently in negotiations from those with unfavourable balances.

The impression that is left from a study of all the agreements is that, in spite of the introduction of the tariff, Britain was still trying to cling to, and even promote, the most-favoured-nation principle in trading relations. Thus the restrictions and/or the easing of them that were introduced through trade agreements did little to alter British trade. They were part of a movement of the time. Snyder examined 510 bilateral conventions, treaties and exchanges of notes for the years 1931–39 and shows how the principle of bilateralism was firmly entrenched as a concept in international trade, something that had come to be regarded as an expedient in a period of economic distress;[10] and Britain was no exception to the movement.

The Exchange Rate

The second factor that requires further comment is the exchange rate. Sterling had been fixed in terms of gold at a rate of $4.86 from April 1925 until September 1931. The story of the return to gold at a slightly overvalued rate in 1925 and of the abandonment of the link with gold in 1931 is well known: the drain on sterling in the summer of 1931 and the rapid depletion of reserves was such that the only sensible decision was to abandon the gold standard and let the pound float to its equilibrium level with other currencies.[11] The immediate consequence was that sterling depreciated quite rapidly such that by the end of the year it was 30 per cent lower in relation to the gold bloc currencies than it had been a matter of three months earlier. However, a number of other countries, particularly primary producers in balance of payments difficulties, had also severed their link with gold during 1930 and 1931.[12] In the course of 1931 most Empire countries followed this lead, though they tended to tie their currency to sterling, and in the twelve months following the British abandonment another twelve countries followed suit. A still further wave of depreciation followed the devaluation of the dollar in 1933. With the devaluation of the dollar, the pound and dollar were back at their former relationship from the end of 1933 onwards. It should be noted, then, that it was only in relation to gold bloc currencies after 1932 that there was much fluctuation, since most sterling area countries tied their currency to the pound. The result was, for example, that in the period from the abandonment in 1931 to the beginning of 1935 there were various movements in the rates and not all in the same direction: an appreciation of 40 per cent of the pound against the dollar, a depreciation of 19 per cent against the French franc, while the currencies of Australia and India fluctuated less than 1 per cent against the pound.

Soon after the abandonment of gold, but before most of these movements could be guessed at, the government attempted to assess the impact (the direction if not the magnitude) of the depreciation on trade variables.[13] The argument was simple: a depreciation of sterling would lead to a reduction of imports through an increase in their sterling price, but this would be offset to some extent by the anticipated depreciation of other countries' currencies; exports would rise, by a similar line of reasoning, but would be offset by the increased price of raw materials. Overall it was not believed possible to make any definite quantitative estimate of the restriction that could be expected as a result of exchange depreciation.

Some indications were sought in an exercise of disappointing simplicity by Customs and Excise.[14] Taking imports in each class of the *Trade and Navigation Accounts* for the calendar year 1929 and for the twelve months immediately prior to the abandonment of gold (1 October 1930 to 30 September 1931) and removing the price effect, they found that there had been an increase of 7 per cent in retained imports of food, drink and tobacco (Class I), a decrease of 17 per cent in raw materials (Class II), and almost no change at all in manufactured goods (Class III). It was felt that the impact of a pound depreciated by something less than 20 per cent, at the time of the investigation in late November 1931, would not substantially alter trade volumes, particularly since many of the most important customers and sources had currencies that moved with sterling. Again using late November as the focal point, they found that there had been a less than 3 per cent variation in the relationship between the pound and the currencies of Scandinavian countries, India and Australasia, amongst others. Most other currencies were at that point about 20 per cent above the gold standard parity,[15] but depreciation by several was correctly anticipated.

Economic historians have never regarded the depreciation of sterling in these years as having had a great effect on trade. For example, Lewis claimed that it had been a profitable episode for only a very brief period,[16] and this judgement has been carried on in the literature since, so that Aldcroft says: ' . . . the advantages [of devaluation] *such as they were*, were very soon whittled away by similar action abroad . . . effectively the British advantages from devaluation lasted only a short time, probably less than two years.'[17]

In the 1970s floating exchange rates directed attention towards the inappropriateness of quoting exchange rates in terms of a numeraire currency, and an improved method of measuring and quoting rates was devised. This has been called the effective rate of exchange and it is a weighted average of one currency against all other currencies, the weights generally being based on the relative trade shares. A recent study extended this technique to the British experience in the 1930s. The results of the exercise are that the pound remained 4 – 5 per cent below the 1929–30 level and 8 per cent below its August 1931 level until well into 1936: 'Thus it would seem that concentration on the pound–dollar rate has led to the benefits of freeing the exchange rate and their role in Britain's recovery being overplayed in 1934–36.'[18]

If then we were to accept Eichengreen's finding (quoted in Chapter 7) that the tariff boosted the exchange rate substantially, and were also to accept the conclusions of the other principal studies on the subject, we would be left with the feeling that the exchange rate was less influential than might have been supposed.

Imperial Preference

As has already been suggested in the survey of the pattern of trade (Chapter 2), as far as total British trade was concerned the impact of imperial preference on trade flows was small, and the effect on British imports was probably less than on exports. But it is worth looking briefly at the origin and development of this feature of policy.

The question of the introduction of imperial preference into the tariff of the United Kingdom was raised at various colonial conferences in the nineteenth century but became a more serious issue in 1907. At that point various parts of the Empire, being highly protectionist, were granting some preferences to the United Kingdom. It was 1917 before any real headway was made on reciprocation, when a resolution in its favour was passed at the Imperial War Conference. As we noted earlier, imperial preference was introduced into the British tariff in the Finance Act of 1919 but the benefits to Empire producers at that stage could only have been very small, depending as they did on the prevailing level of duties in Britain. It should also be remembered that a primary aim of preference (which applied of course almost exclusively to primary produce) was the stimulation of production in the Empire. The observations of the Board of Customs were that except in the case of tobacco the stimulus to increased production had probably not been large.[19] It is not difficult to see why, either in aggregate or for individual commodities. The total of the preferential rebate on dutiable goods imported into Britain in 1928/9 was less than £8m.; 85 per cent of that was made up of rebates on sugar, tobacco and tea.[20]

The products that benefited most came from the Colonies and India rather than the Dominions, yet it had been the latter that had raised the issue most urgently in 1917, pressed it most forcefully in 1923, and lobbied relentlessly throughout the 1920s for greater preferential trading arrangements. Of course it is clear that, in the absence of preference, a great deal of trade would have taken place anyway, as a consequence either of other advantages or of a lack of substitution possibilities. In any case it would require a sophisticated analysis to estimate the 'trade-creating' and 'trade-diverting' effects of preferential tariffs.

There is really only one *industry* that enjoyed preferential rates that was significant to a Dominion (Canada) and to Britain and that was the motor car industry. This industry was protected by the McKenna duties throughout the 1920s, with a brief lapse in 1924/5. The import of Canadian cars into Britain increased in 1919 when the first preference was granted, production being diverted across the border to Canada from the United States. Cars of Empire origin (effectively Canadian) made up 4 per cent of total imports of cars in 1920/1, but this rose steadily to around 36 per cent before the duties were abolished in 1924. The abolition of the tariff led to a reduction in imports from Canada and an increase in those from America. The obvious explanation is that under the duties the American firms of General Motors and Chrysler, who manufactured on both sides of the Canadian/United States border, used Canadian factories to cater for trade with the British Empire. With the reintroduction of the McKenna duties in 1925, the Empire proportion began to rise again and it stabilised at around 20 per cent of the import market in the later 1920s. However, it was the British view in 1930 that, since the Canadian industry had a worldwide market, 'it may be inferred that [while] production in Canada has been increased by Preference ... the point cannot be strongly pressed'.[21]

Although it is difficult to measure precisely the effects of preferences, it is clear that, as far as any balance sheet between the Dominions and the United Kingdom goes, up to 1930 the former conferred greater benefits on the United Kingdom than they gained.[22] Against this however, as the British authorities were always eager to point out, there were several other measures that in effect bestowed a reasonable benefit on the Dominions – factors such as the provision of cheap capital for developed projects, or the bearing of the great bulk of the burden of naval defence of the Empire. More comparable was the work of the Empire Marketing Board and its promotion of Empire produce in Britain.

In the 1930s opportunities for some extension of preference came with the introduction of the general tariff, but the fact remains that the Empire was still overwhelmingly a primary-producing bloc and the opportunities for such extension were limited. As far as the industrial tariff went, imperial preference continued to have little importance outside of the car industry and a small number of 'key industries'. Preferential arrangements were of course extended in the 1930s to the Dominions (through quotas) on their important exports such as meat. There were also other, longer-term and unquantifiable effects of preference. One notable one was the bitterness it introduced into trading relations with the United States. Ultimately the United States insisted (as part of the lend-lease arrangements made during the Second World War) that imperial preference be disbanded.

To sum up. It is reasonable that the three factors briefly discussed in this chapter should be thought of as potentially important elements in any consideration of the tariff, but the evidence suggests that their significance was rather modest. Nothing of interest or importance arose out of the bulk of the trade negotiations and agreements that followed the introduction of the tariff. Equally, the calculation of the effective rate of exchange points to the fact that this variable had little impact on trade flows. Imperial preference, by virtue of its nature and size, could affect only a tiny portion of industrial output and manufactured imports.

Notes

1 Public Record Office, T 160/445/F12919/7, Import Duties Bill.
2 ibid.
3 ibid.
4 A detailed treatment of this agreement can be found in R. Gravil and T. Rooth, 'A Time of Acute Dependence: Argentina in the 1930s', *Journal of European Economic History* (1978), pp. 337–78.
5 Public Record Office, T 160/494/13090/02/3, Tariff Negotiations.
6 ibid.
7 *British Parliamentary Papers*, 1933–4, *Exchange of Notes Between HM Govern-*

ment of the UK and the French Government Respecting Commercial Relations, Cmd 4590.

8 J. Henry Richardson, 'Tariffs, Preferences and Other Forms of Protection', British Association, *Britain in Recovery* (1938), p. 131.
9 Public Record Office, T 160/445/F12919/7, op.cit.
10 R. C. Snyder, 'Commercial Policy as Reflected in Treaties from 1931–1939', *American Economic Review* (1940).
11 Not quite its true equilibrium level since there was still a considerable amount of activity by the Bank of England in the foreign exchange market.
12 Argentina had left as early as December 1929.
13 Public Record Office, CAB 27/467, January 1932, Committee on Balance of Trade.
14 Reported in CAB 27/467.
15 ibid.
16 W. A. Lewis, *Economic Survey, 1919–1935* (1949), p. 82.
17 Derek H. Aldcroft, *The Inter-war Economy: Britain 1919–1939* (1970), p. 281, emphasis added.
18 John Redmond, 'An Indicator of the Effective Rate of the Pound in the Nineteen Thirties', *Economic History Review* (1980), p. 88.
19 Public Record Office, CAB 58/149, Appendix H, Imperial Preference.
20 ibid.
21 ibid., p. 23.
22 For a fairly thorough assessment of what preference meant for the Empire in the 1930s, see Ian M. Drummond, *Imperial Economic Policy 1917–1939* (1974); and for some detailed estimates for individual commodities see F. V. Meyer, *Britain's Colonies in World Trade* (1948).

10

Conclusion

The British abandonment of free trade in 1932 was a significant event in international economic affairs. As we have noted, Britain was the birthplace and, since the 1840s, effectively the principal upholder and exporter of the free trade doctrine. She was also, of course, still one of the world's leading trading nations. When she then became the last major trader to capitulate to the protectionist pressure (both domestic and international), this signalled an important turning point.

This book has analysed the origins and effects of Britain's industrial tariff legislation between the wars. While there are revisions to conventional views on specific parts of the topic, the principal focus has been an exploration of neglected territory – the economic aspects of the origins of the tariff and its domestic economic effects. In this study, business interest is the thread linking origins and effects. The object has been to examine the economic and commercial role in the breakdown of free trade policy and then to look at the effects on industry. This has been set against the background of a political and social climate that was favourable to a change in a hostile world.

At one extreme, the origins of the general tariff can be sought in the protectionist movements of the late nineteenth century and opening years of the twentieth century; at the other extreme, the tariff can be seen as a panic response to the economic depression of 1929–32. The argument has been that, in spite of protestations over 'dumping' and the supposed need for immediate protection from 'abnormal' imports in 1931, the beginnings of the reversal of British free trade policy are to be found in the years from the First World War onwards, when certain interests, working in a climate of international distrust and economic sluggishness, accelerated the protectionist case. The principal source of pressure is found in the activity of sections of the business community. The iron and steel industry has been shown to have been a particularly insistent force, and the unique contribution of the Empire Industries Association illustrates a very important aspect of business activity in Parliament. The point to stress, however, is that the pressure seems to have built up steadily over the years, although allowance must be made for competing interests and for gains and losses being made along the way.[1] There is no way of demonstrating conclusively that the pressures described contributed to the introduction of the tariff in 1932, but some support is found in the fact that government was well aware of the pressures and particularly of the insidious form they could take in the continuing changes to the tariff structure. Having decided on a protectionist commercial policy, government then tried to remove itself from the more direct pressures that it correctly anticipated would follow. The Import Duties Advisory Committee was the means of achieving neutrality and our analysis of the operation of this buffer does suggest that government was moderately successful on this score, though this refers only to the *structure* of the tariff. The tariff could never be taken wholly out of politics, and an agency such as IDAC would have been authorised to continue only so long as it carried out the broad policy of government.

When trying to assess the degree of protection afforded to British industry in the 1930s, it is not very helpful to look at the heights of the various nominal tariffs imposed in 1932 and in subsequent revisions. It is the effective protection rate that shows by how much the value-added in an industry can exceed the value-added in the absence of protection. Since there was an awareness of this concept in the business world at the time, an examination of the effective tariff structure aids an understanding of the working of business groups in their pursuit of tariff legislation. It is also the appropriate structure to examine when determining how the tariff came to reach its final form. The results of this part of the enquiry were that the structure was influenced not by the large and powerful industries but instead by the smaller and more needy and by regional considerations. One primary objective of the Import Duties Advisory Committee was to protect the most vulnerable industries from foreign competition as indicated by some measure of import penetration, but this does not appear to have been achieved.

The effects of the tariff have received varied treatment over the years. When the Chancellor of the Exchequer, Neville Chamberlain, introduced the protectionist legislation in 1932 he was confident that it would prove an important turning point in British economic and political history:

When some day the historian comes to set on record his view of the events of February 1932, I believe he will point to that date as one of the landmarks in the strange and eventful history of our race. I believe he will applaud and admire the courage and the foresight of this country...[2]

Chamberlain did not wait for the historians to revise this view. His remarks made at the beginning of 1940 are worth quoting at length for they suggest a fairly comprehensive turnabout from his earlier position and perhaps there is a recognition of some lessons learnt from the experience between 1932 and 1939. This latter point should not be overplayed, however, for he was undoubtedly subject to strong pressures from the United States at the time the remarks were made.

... the most favoured nation clause, a principle which in our view in normal times was the best way of promoting international trade. And we mean when this work is successfully concluded to return to that idea. We recognise that for the full development of international trade it must flow along multilateral channels, and that we must put an end to that vicious policy of economic nationalism and autarky which did so much to upset the last great peace settlement. One of our foremost aims will be the restoration of international trade, which seems to us to present the best opportunity for restoring in turn the standard of living and the consuming power of nations.[3]

In terms of what Chamberlain was looking for on the economic front, the tariff can hardly be considered a success. Tariffs can have several different effects and some types of analysis are more appropriate for some than for others. For example, the effect on prices and output can be approximated through the partial equilibrium analysis by representing the demand and supply schedules for certain goods. This approach has been used in this study, and while it yields some results of interest, the limitations of the exercise are clear. The most interesting results are those that came out of the examination of effective rates of protection, which point to the likely impact on the direction of resource flows that the tariff would have had. The clear conclusion here is that, since the two biggest sectors (construction and iron and steel) generally accredited with the principal contribution to economic recovery had very low effective rates of protection, the tariff played an insignificant part in the upturn out of depression. Indeed, the role in stimulating the manufacturing sector in the 1930s must have been small.

The study has concentrated on the domestic economy and at no stage has it pretended to account for international repercussions. One of the more obvious of these was retaliation. There is a vast literature in international trade theory that deals with retaliation but it is almost always an analysis of the consequences, developed out of the theory of optimum tariffs, and not an analysis of the cause of retaliation. At one level this is not surprising since retaliation is frequently assumed to be irrational and the effects are all that can sensibly be analysed. But there are examples of considered and measured retaliatory responses that might usefully be analysed. The lack of attention to the topic in this study is largely a result of the conscious focusing on the domestic economy, but partly also the result of lack of agreement in the theory and its empirical possibilities. For example, Johnson claims that orthodox international trade theory is incapable of explaining the phenomenon of tariff bargaining,[4] though recently an attempt at revising that view has been put forward.[5]

In some senses of course the British tariff was itself retaliatory and, in the response that followed it, I have taken account of some of the tariff negotiations. Trade negotiations between Britain and some trading partners did take place but the tentative conclusion must be that these were not of significance for the total trading pattern. It was Jacob Viner's conclusion at the time that, with the exception of the period 1860–75, tariff bargaining had never successfully lowered barriers to trade; indeed, if anything, it had contributed to raising them.[6]

An aim of many of the imperialist protectionists was a self-sufficient Empire. This had been the principal objective of such groups as Beaverbrook's Empire Free Trade campaigners, apparently combining the appeal of loyalty and free trade in one basket but in fact being a vehicle for the introduction of protection. Here, too, there is no case to be made for the tariff having promoted such a scheme. The notion of a large trading area with tariffs to outsiders and preferential arrangements for members was given some academic respectability from a slightly unexpected quarter[7] – the book by Beveridge and other free traders at the London School of Economics designed to influence British public opinion against protection.[8] Beveridge and Hicks set out the case for a customs union as follows:

The essence of protection is the discouragement of imports. The essence of preferential trade is the encouragement of some imports rather than others, with a view to securing a market for exports. Protection negatives international trade. Preference aims at developing international trade by giving it assured channels. In this extreme form of a customs union with a high tariff against the rest of the world, but no barriers within the union, arrangements for preference may be viewed as the most practical way of securing the largest possible measure of free trade . . . They may be urged at this juncture as the only way of securing for Britain something like the place in the economic structure of the world that was envisaged for her by the founders of her fiscal policy.[9]

But of course the Empire tariff arrangements of 1932 were far removed from a customs union. There was no common tariff barrier and no common preferential arrangements, but rather a rag-bag of agreements. In any case, while it may have sounded sensible for a primary producer to form a union with an industrial country, theory and practice suggest that primary producers should form customs union with themselves and industrial countries with others like themselves. Under these circumstances the scope for trade creation is greatest.

Much of what we have seen in this examination of protectionism in the interwar years has some striking similarities with the last decade or so. For example, pressure for protection, and protection itself, grew steadily in the 1920s, culminating in the breakdown of international trade in the depression of the 1930s. And a further burst of retaliatory measures contributed to the failure of trade to recover and so to the prolonged world recession. While in the middle of the 1960s some small protectionist measures did still exist (notably against the United States' exports of agricultural produce to Europe), the 1950s and 1960s were generally years of free trade and rapid economic growth. But by the 1970s, with economic growth faltering in many countries, the range of goods being protected and countries adopting protection was increasing enormously.

The main thrust of this pressure for protection can be dated from the downturn of the mid 1970s and demands grew steadily thereafter, with the greatest increase coming in the deepening world depression of 1979–83. This recent movement has been dubbed the new protectionism. Those who wish to avoid the term employ euphemisms to take attention away from what is nevertheless protection; 'orderly trade' and 'managed trade' are two of the more popular.

Another similarity between the interwar years and the 1970s and 1980s lies in the great number of world economic summit meetings. In the interwar years the League of Nations organised the meetings and worked diligently to promote cooperation; in the 1970s and 1980s GATT has provided the forum. But the experience in both cases was very similar: while the participants at the international level in both periods invariably agreed on the need to resist protectionist pressures and promote greater international trading cooperation, on the domestic front the pressures for protection were too great for governments to resist.

Other parallels could be drawn out, and of course there are differences too, between the two experiences. Lessons from the past, if they exist, are far from unambiguous, but the experience of the interwar years adds to our general understanding of the issue of protectionism and its course and outcome. The principal causes have again been seen to be war and economic depression, and when the pressure develops there is little that international organisations can do to dispel its force. Further, there is little evidence that protection has ever done anything to promote economic growth and welfare, and the interwar experience provides further evidence of that. Indeed, the growth of protectionism has invariably gone hand in hand with developing nationalism, and imperialism, and resulted in dismal consequences.

Notes

1 The picture presented here is at odds with the view of Middlemas that something called corporatism developed in these years – i.e. that capital, labour and government worked together in search of the best road forward. Keith Middlemas, *Politics in Industrial Society* (1979). This is not the place to challenge the view of Middlemas, but simply to point out the difference; an alternative stance can be found in J. A. Turner, 'The British Commonwealth Union and the General Election of 1918', *The English Historical Review* (1978).
2 *British Parliamentary Papers*, 1931–32, *Commons Debates*, Vol. 262, Col. 712.
3 Quoted in D. R. E. Abel, *A History of British Tariffs 1923–1942* (1945), p. 134.
4 Harry G. Johnson, 'An Economic Theory of Protectionism, Tariff Bargaining and the Formation of Customs Union', *Journal of Political Economy* (1965).
5 Ali El-Agraa, 'On Optimum Tariffs, Retaliation, International Co-operation and Tariff Bargaining', *Bulletin of Economic Research* (1979).
6 Jacob Viner, 'Economic Thought: Mercantilist Thought', *International Encyclopedia of the Social Sciences*, Vol. 4 (1934).
7 The London School of Economics lost its protectionist and imperialist connection and became the centre for the free trade argument.
8 Sir William Beveridge *et al.*, *Tariffs: the Case Examined* (1932). See Chapter 4 for some of the story behind the little volume.
9 ibid., p. 135.

Appendix

This appendix gives details on how the series of British imports of raw materials, semi-manufactured and manufactured goods for the years 1925–36 were deseasonalised.[1] There are several purposes for which such series can be used in an examination of trade flows, but the specific problem here is the unravelling of the extent of what were called, at the time, 'abnormal' imports into Britain of various product groups, particularly late in 1931. The answer to this question can throw light on the degree of 'dumping' or buying in anticipation of the tariff that was claimed by contemporaries to be so prevalent.[2] The approach used is to employ recently developed deseasonalising techniques to remove seasonality from the raw data and then to calculate any irregular deviation from the remaining trend.

Thirty-four monthly series of commodity groups in Classes II and III of the *Trade and Navigation Accounts*, together with Class totals for Classes I, II and III and the total of all imports, were selected (see Table A.1).[3] The length of the period is of importance since in estimating seasonality we wish to be sure that we have a period long enough to capture typical seasonal movements but not so long as to embrace a change in the seasonal pattern.

Several procedures are available for seasonally adjusting data, each based on different conceptual mechanisms according to varying assumptions concerning the seasonal behaviour of the data. For example, if we assume additive seasonality, seasonal adjustment involves estimating seasonal effects and subtracting them from the observed data. An alternative, and more common, assumption is that seasonal effects are proportional to trend. In other words, seasonality is multiplicative. Seasonal adjustment in this case involves estimating the factors and dividing the original series by them. Most techniques in the past have involved using one of these two options. Obviously behaviour can be more complicated than these options allow for; a mixture of both additive and multiplicative elements may be present, or over a period the nature of seasonality may change. It is clearly desirable to obtain the 'cleanest' deseasonalised series possible in order to avoid attributing to a random factor (like 'anticipatory buying') something that is in fact seasonal, or vice versa. Recently improved deseasonalising has been made possible by developments at the Central Statistical Office (CSO).[4] It is their seasonal adjustment programme and their model test programme that were used in this exercise.

Before using the seasonal adjustment programme, however, the first step is to ascertain which of the series contain seasonal elements. This can be moderately successfully achieved by graphing all the series and assessing each visually. However a more rigorous test is available – that of analysis of variance.[5] I used a two-way analysis of variance, between years and between months, testing the hypothesis that no trend or seasonal variation was

Table A.1 *Trade Series Investigated for Seasonality*

	Code
Class II:	
Coal	WA
Other non-metalliferous mining	WB
Iron ore and scrap	WC
Non-ferrous metalliferous ores	WD
Wood and timber	WE
Raw cotton and cotton waste	WF
Raw wool	WG
Silk	WH
Other textile materials	WI
Seeds and nuts for oils, etc.	WJ
Hides and skins	WK
Paper making materials	WL
Rubber	WM
Miscellaneous raw materials	WN
Class III:	
Coke and manufactured fuel	XA
Earthenware, glass, abrasives, etc.	XB
Iron and steel manufactures	XC
Non-ferrous metals and manufactures	XD
Cutlery, hardware, etc.	XE
Electrical goods and apparatus	XF
Machinery	XG
Manufactures of wood and timber	XH
Cotton yarns and manufactures	XI
Woollen and worsted manufactures	XJ
Silk and silk manufactures	XK
Manufactures of other materials	XL
Apparel and footwear	XM
Chemicals, drugs, dyes and colours	XN
Oils, fats and resins, manufactured	XO
Leather and manufactures	XP
Paper and cardboard	XQ
Vehicles	XR
Rubber manufactures	XS
Miscellaneous manufactures	XT
Class I total (food etc.)	V
Class II total (raw materials)	W
Class III total (manufactures)	X
Total imports	M

present. The F-ratios were calculated in the customary way and are provided in Table A.2. As a check on this routine, I retested the derived deseasonalised series and obtained wholly insignificant F-ratios, thus satisfying the query over any remaining seasonality.

Where seasonality was found to be present I then employed the CSO seasonal adjustment programme. The first part is to use the model test programme.[6] This enables the user to decide whether an additive, multiplicative or combined model is required as the basis for seasonal adjustment. Briefly the technique is as follows.[7] The initial assumption is that the series has three components: trend, seasonal and irregular. Trend is estimated, and then over a period of years the deviations from trend are regressed against a set of additive seasonal factors. Then over the same period the deviations are regressed against a set of both additive and multiplicative factors. If there were a significant increase in the explained sum of squares with the introduction of multiplicative terms then the latter were regarded as necessary for correct adjustment. The process is then repeated starting with a multiplicative model and introducing additive terms.

Several outcomes are possible, and can be read from the variance ratio test in the output of the model test programme. It may be that either model (additive or multiplicative) would produce satisfactory results. But it may be that only additive or only multiplicative terms are needed. It is also possible that both terms are required. Table A.3 provides the results of the model test programme for our series. It can be seen that for most series either a multiplicative or an additive model is sufficient. On only two occasions was a mixed model prescribed.

Table A.2   *Results of Variance Analysis*

| | F-ratio | |
Series code	Between months	Between years
WA	.727 (.999)	9.118 (.001)
WB	2.156 (.021)	38.218 (.001)
WC	3.149 (.001)	34.231 (.001)
WD	3.424 (.001)	44.791 (.001)
WE	98.669 (.001)	23.036 (.001)
WF	10.203 (.001)	27.023 (.001)
WG	43.024 (.001)	19.486 (.001)
WH	4.515 (.001)	3.059 (.001)
WI	18.977 (.001)	10.620 (.001)
WJ	4.176 (.001)	100.429 (.001)
WK	12.489 (.001)	31.512 (.001)
WL	17.258 (.001)	10.005 (.001)
WM	.951 (.999)	27.406 (.001)
WN	38.805 (.001)	25.876 (.001)
XA	1.007 (.445)	5.084 (.001)
XB	8.732 (.001)	72.526 (.001)
XC	.872 (.999)	59.714 (.001)
XD	1.813 (.058)	44.458 (.001)

Table A.2 *continued*

Series code	F-ratio	
	Between months	*Between years*
XE	2.654 (.005)	11.166 (.001)
XF	11.710 (.001)	37.229 (.001)
XG	2.685 (.001)	48.662 (.001)
XH	1.925 (.042)	26.497 (.001)
XI	4.434 (.001)	238.150 (.001)
XJ	4.125 (.001)	172.727 (.001)
XK	1.297 (.234)	21.413 (.001)
XL	1.909 (.044)	49.769 (.001)
XM	7.364 (.001)	80.778 (.001)
XN	3.126 (.001)	19.727 (.001)
XO	2.465 (.008)	14.228 (.001)
XP	2.170 (.020)	53.475 (.001)
XQ	7.697 (.001)	17.759 (.001)
XR	2.100 (.025)	26.635 (.001)
XS	3.737 (.001)	18.378 (.001)
XT	11.503 (.001)	88.977 (.001)
V	18.358 (.001)	138.778 (.001)
W	12.053 (.001)	89.082 (.001)
X	1.962 (.038)	104.818 (.001)
M	3.470 (.001)	38.646 (.001)

(1) No marked seasonal variation:

WA	Coal	XA	Coke	XL	Other manfrs.
WB	Non-metalli-ferous metals	XC	Iron & steel manfrs.	XN	Chemicals
WC	Iron ore	XD	Non-ferrous manfrs.	XO	Oils, fats
WD	Non-ferrous metals			XP	Leather manfrs.
		XE	Cutlery	XR	Vehicles
WH	Silk	XG	Machinery	XS	Rubber manfrs.
WJ	Seeds & nuts	XH	Wood manfrs.		
WM	Rubber				
X	All Class III				
M	All Imports				

(2) Clearly marked seasonal variation:

WE	Wood & timber	WK	Hides & skins
WF	Raw cotton	WL	Paper making materials
WG	Raw wool	WN	Misc. raw materials
WI	Other textiles	XF	Electrical goods
V	All Class I	XT	Misc. manufactures
W	All Class II		

(3) Seasonal variation and irregular movement:

XB	Earthenware
XQ	Paper & cardboard
XI	Cotton yarn manfrs.
XJ	Woollen yarn manfrs.
XM	Apparel and footwear

Table A.3 *Type of Model Required as Determined by Model Test Programme*

WE	Multiplicative
WF	Multiplicative
WG	Multiplicative
WH	Multiplicative
WK	Multiplicative
WL	Additive
WN	Additive
XB	Additive
XF	Multiplicative
XI	Either
XJ	Mixed
XM	Mixed
XQ	Additive
XT	Either
V	Multiplicative
W	Multiplicative

One minor complication that arose in some cases and had to be resolved was that of an abrupt break in trend. It was apparent simply from looking at the graphs for the series that some suffered from such a break whose typical pattern can be characterised as in Figure A.1. If such a break in trend were ignored it would distort the calculation of seasonality. There are various means of handling the problem but the one adopted in this instance was the following. The trend t_1 was extrapolated (t_1^1) and the difference between t_1^1

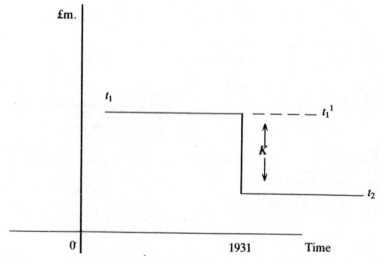

Figure A.1

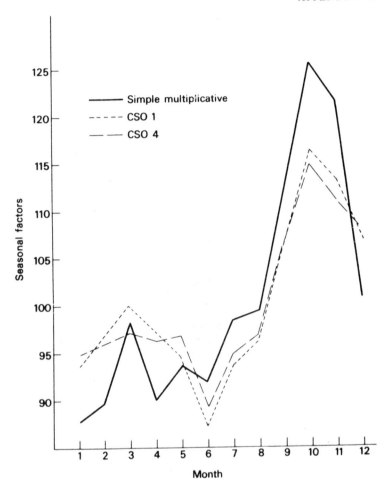

Figure A.2a   Seasonal Factors for Cotton Yarns and Manufactures

and t_2, the constant K, calculated. K was then added to each of the raw values in the series from December 1931 onwards and this reconstructed series was then processed through the model test programme and the best seasonal model selected. This model was used to produce a deseasonalised series (which of course still included the value K). Finally K was removed from this series to obtain the 'true' deseasonalised series. Deviations from the trend were then calculated in the customary fashion by deducting this true series from a 21-point moving average of the original data.

Table A.4 contains the final results of this exercise – the percentage deviations from the trend values of the deseasonalised series. It can be seen

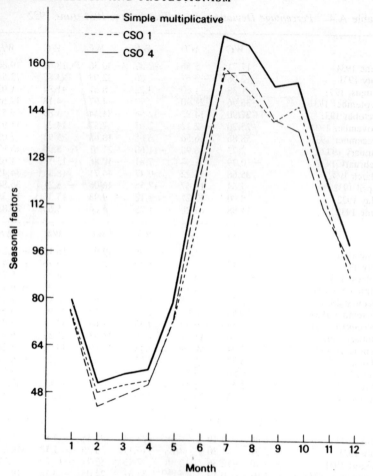

Figure A.2b   Seasonal Factors for Wood and Timber

from these results that there was no significant increase in raw material imports (Class II) in October and November 1931. But when we turn to Class III groups we find cases where purchases were over 100 per cent higher than 'expected'.

One additional point might be made. When the seasonal factors produced by this method are compared with previous methods no great differences are observed, though there are sufficient variations to provide justification for the more elaborate testing procedure. Figure A.2 provides some illustrations of the results of both the CSO approach and simpler straightforward multiplicative model. (CSO1 and CSO4 are the multiplicative and mixed models, respectively.)

Table A.4   *Percentage Deviations from Trend, June 1931–June 1932*

	WC	WD	WE	WF	WG	WH
June 1931	17.71	5.66	−2.82	30.36	18.68	19.80
July 1931	2.06	−5.67	7.86	32.04	3.82	−13.54
August 1931	−1.38	−1.60	0.22	8.67	−41.84	−1.03
September 1931	−36.96	−24.90	−7.77	−4.97	−4.13	17.65
October 1931	−27.90	−14.92	−12.56	−34.44	5.89	−9.52
November 1931	−25.20	− 2.12	− 2.05	7.57	14.23	−11.93
December 1931	58.86	16.50	6.65	10.65	5.95	7.08
January 1932	2.73	6.90	−11.60	−21.61	− 8.94	−15.97
February 1932	− 0.39	1.34	7.81	−10.86	−13.13	− 1.65
March 1932	35.68	15.22	0.47	44.71	18.33	34.45
April 1932	− 5.64	10.67	−17.55	16.06	− 8.21	36.84
May 1932	8.00	12.21	1.12	− 9.93	15.35	15.38
June 1932	11.88	7.28	1.75	4.64	5.63	20.83

	WI	WJ	WK	WL	WM	WN
June 1931	33.87	3.02	− 3.68	−19.95	−16.15	− 2.23
July 1931	20.13	−11.35	− 5.49	12.72	−10.76	− 3.42
August 1931	−15.02	− 6.02	− 5.39	−11.66	−18.33	5.72
September 1931	19.45	−20.18	−17.08	− 0.23	−28.95	−10.14
October 1931	6.95	−17.51	1.47	6.63	16.42	−11.11
November 1931	−11.59	− 0.07	1.70	− 2.12	−22.09	14.63
December 1931	5.59	− 9.56	− 0.35	7.69	33.73	3.07
January 1932	2.46	11.71	1.24	11.53	21.55	− 6.91
February 1932	− 7.04	50.69	10.48	11.89	40.01	− 5.20
March 1932	− 8.77	1.58	17.71	− 3.42	− 1.19	− 6.16
April 1932	−30.90	9.10	−12.00	−10.93	1.23	−12.70
May 1932	−12.17	− 8.38	− 7.13	− 7.48	−12.82	−11.26
June 1932	− 7.53	−10.85	18.93	− 9.37	− 6.69	− 0.46

	XB	XF	XI	XJ	XM	XQ	XT
June 1931	− 6.46	− 0.19	− 0.88	−28.84	−37.58	2.80	1.77
July 1931	− 3.37	1.30	3.88	−10.19	6.55	− 1.73	10.85
August 1931	− 7.16	−12.36	3.18	7.13	12.77	−11.09	15.22
September 1931	− 1.93	− 0.19	21.08	37.51	24.08	− 3.26	19.36
October 1931	24.06	19.74	34.84	82.01	22.13	13.90	18.08
November 1931	38.78	88.77	56.79	118.34	41.22	17.28	23.28
December 1931	−25.37	−36.91	−40.12	−61.87	−32.83	− 4.89	−24.40
January 1932	−19.17	−43.89	−54.91	−70.69	−46.75	−10.08	−19.17
February 1932	42.98	−13.00	−48.55	−70.57	−13.67	17.33	−11.76
March 1932	−20.42	−36.54	−61.64	−68.81	−30.96	− 0.57	−22.37
April 1932	−24.04	− 7.99	−44.81	−81.45	−21.56	− 8.65	−17.63
May 1932	−10.02	−18.66	− 6.67	4.61	− 3.21	− 0.78	−17.09
June 1932	− 2.42	12.50	111.03	18.49	13.40	− 7.89	−12.76

Table A.4 *continued*

	XC	XD	XE	XG	XH	XK
June 1931	− 2.45	− 7.27	9.40	− 5.13	0.30	−12.29
July 1931	− 6.82	− 2.33	− 6.91	− 6.04	− 5.55	−11.44
August 1931	−19.51	−19.45	−26.13	−20.50	− 6.11	1.99
September 1931	−10.96	−12.05	1.95	−21.05	−12.29	31.89
October 1931	17.23	14.51	59.47	34.57	9.14	38.29
November 1931	71.16	28.64	105.55	39.34	20.10	20.43
December 1931	19.71	13.93	−19.69	5.20	18.10	−24.43
January 1932	−22.79	−15.16	−52.89	−21.34	3.48	−39.40
February 1932	24.70	60.88	−30.31	38.05	18.18	−13.02
March 1932	−26.49	− 0.78	−31.49	−17.29	− 2.27	6.83
April 1932	−26.14	−45.06	−16.80	−24.27	−18.59	31.58
May 1932	−23.98	−28.38	− 7.88	3.18	− 5.48	−22.38
June 1932	−24.15	−27.04	− 3.00	− 3.71	− 8.95	− 1.58

	XL	XN	XO	XP	XR	XS
June 1931	−11.86	−20.09	3.45	− 9.76	−28.10	−21.86
July 1931	− 4.43	−19.37	− 5.98	−12.13	−26.07	−16.18
August 1931	− 2.88	−14.26	− 6.80	−15.58	−24.96	− 5.30
September 1931	10.08	−14.82	−17.80	−10.49	151.31	4.53
October 1931	33.72	37.73	13.10	37.80	41.94	57.40
November 1931	39.11	63.50	− 8.76	58.01	− 4.90	46.98
December 1931	−24.38	7.25	4.98	− 3.25	−49.83	− 7.37
January 1932	−32.08	−25.86	− 1.28	−25.41	−46.40	−55.95
February 1932	5.34	49.91	26.29	57.37	−10.45	− 5.72
March 1932	2.31	−16.09	− 6.57	−25.50	27.26	−10.61
April 1932	− 1.45	−40.85	3.89	−29.50	14.26	− 4.01
May 1932	−25.80	−38.67	− 6.86	−35.24	4.90	−27.09
June 1932	−13.77	−26.73	4.88	−28.21	−17.69	−11.37

Notes

1   I should like to thank David Harkness for all the help he gave on the preparation of this Appendix.
2   Obviously there are other problems involved in isolating the anticipatory effects of buying ahead of the tariff as against the depreciation of sterling, which was going on at the same time.
3   The data are taken from *Accounts Relating to the Trade and Navigation of the United Kingdom* (monthly), 1925–36.
4   M. J. Murphy, *The CSO Mixed Model for Seasonal Adjustment (Brown's Method) and Model-Test Programmes*, Research Exercise Note 5/73 (1973).
5   A useful description of this is provided in C. E. V. Leser, *Seasonality in Irish Economic Statistics*, Institute for Economic and Social Research, Paper No. 26 (1965).
6   An excellent non-technical account is provided in P. B. Kenny, 'Problems of Seasonal Adjustment', *Statistical News* (1975); a technical account can be found in J. Durbin and M. J. Murphy, 'Seasonal Adjustment based on a Mixed Additive–Multiplicative Model', *Journal of the Royal Statistical Society* (1975).
7   This paraphrases some of Durbin and Murphy, op.cit.

Bibliography

Abel, Deryck, *The British Free Trade View of Empire Preference* (London, Free Trade Union, no date).

Abel, Deryck, *A History of British Tariffs, 1923–1942* (London, Heath Granton, 1945).

Accounts Relating to the Trade and Navigation of the United Kingdom (London, HMSO).

Aldcroft, Derek H., *The Inter-War Economy: Britain 1919–1939* (London, Batsford, 1970).

Allen, G. C., *A Short Economic History of Modern Japan, 1867–1937* (London, Allen & Unwin, 1972).

Allen, R. G. D., *International Trade Statistics* (London, Chapman & Hall, 1953).

Amery, L. S., *The Fundamental Fallacies of Free Trade* (London, National Review, 1906).

Amery, L. S., *My Political Life. Vol. II, War and Peace 1914–1929* (London, Hutchinson, 1953–5).

Amery, L. S., *My Political Life. Vol. III, The Unforgiving Years 1929–40* (London, Hutchinson, 1955).

Annual Statement of Trade of the United Kingdom with Commonwealth Countries and Foreign Countries (London, HMSO).

Arndt, H. W., *The Economic Lessons of the Nineteen Thirties* (London, Oxford University Press, 1944).

Arnold, Lord, *The Safeguarding of Steel: Fallacies Exposed* (June 1931).

Ashley, Percy, 'An Experiment in Tariff Making', *Manchester School*, Vol. XI, No.2 (April 1940).

Ashley, W. J., *The Tariff Problem* (New York, Kelley, 1903).

Asquith, Cyril, *The Failure of Protection* (Liberal Free Trade Committee, October 1934).

Awad, F. H., 'Structure of the World Export Trade 1926–1953', *Yorkshire Bulletin* Vol. II (1959).

Baden-Powell, Sir George, 'The Development of Tropical Africa', *Proceedings Royal Col. Institute*, Vol. 27 (1895–6).

Balassa, Bela, 'Tariff Protection in Industrial Countries: An Evaluation', *Journal of Political Economy* (December 1965).

Balassa, Bela, *et al.*, *The Structure of Protection in Developing Countries* (Baltimore, Md, Johns Hopkins University Press, 1971).

Baldwin, R. E., 'Commodity Composition of World Trade, 1900–1954', *Review of Economics and Statistics* (1958).

Barker, T., 'Aggregation Error and Estimates of the U.S. Import Demand Function', *The Econometric Study of the United Kingdom*, (London, Macmillan, 1970).

Barker, T. C., *Pilkington Brothers and the Glass Industry* (London, G. Allen, 1960).

Barker, T. S. and Han, S. S., 'Effective Rates of Protection for United Kingdom Production', *Economic Journal*, Vol. 81, (June 1971), pp. 282–93.

Barna, T., 'The Interdependence of the British Economy', *Journal of the Royal Statistical Society*, Part I (1952), pp. 29–77.

Basevi, G., 'The United States Tariff Structure: Estimates of Effective Rates of Protection of United States Industries and Industrial Labour', *Review of Economics and Statistics*, (1966).

Beaverbrook, Lord, 'Empire Free Trade', *Daily Express* (1930).

Beaverbrook Papers (House of Lords).

Beer, Samuel H., *Modern British Politics* (London, Faber, 1969).

Benham, F. C. C., *Great Britain Under Protection* (New York, Macmillan, 1941).

Beresford, M. W., *The Leeds Chamber of Commerce* (Leeds, Leeds Chamber of Commerce, 1951).

Beveridge, William H., *Empire Free Trade, A Reply to Lord Beaverbrook* (London, Longman, 1931).

Beveridge, W., *et al.*, *Tariffs: The Case Examined* (London, Longman, 1932).

Beveridge Papers (British Library of Political and Economic Science).

Botha, D. J. J., 'On Tariff Policy: The Formative Years', *South African Journal of Economics*, Vol. 41, No.4 (December 1973), pp. 231–55.

Boyd, C. W. (ed.), *Chamberlain's Speeches* (London, Constable, 1914).

Breton, A., *The Economic Theory of Representative Government* (London, Macmillan, 1974).

Brigden, J. B., *et al.*, *The Australian Tariff – An Economic Enquiry* (Melbourne University Press, 1929).

British Association, *Britain in Recovery* (London, Pitman, 1938).

British Iron and Steel Federation (London, The Federation, 1963).

British Parliamentary Papers, 1872, Vol. LXIII, Accounts and Papers 28, No.1;

 1916, Vol. LXII, Accounts and Papers No. 3;

 1914–16, Vol., LXV, Accounts and Papers No. 3.

 1901, *Foreign Import Duties*, Cd. 780, Vol. LXXX, p. 519.

 1903, *Foreign Import Duties*, Cd. 1735, Vol. LXXI, p. 1.

 1912–13, *Foreign Import Duties 1912*, Cd. 6475, Vol. LXXXIV, p. 1.

 1917, *Dominions Commission*, Cd. 8642, Vol. LXXXVIII.

 1918, *Final Report of the Committee on Commercial and Industrial Policy After the War*, Cd. 9035, Vol. XIII, p. 239.

 1918, *Report of the Departmental Committee appointed by the Board of Trade to consider the position of Iron and Steel Trade after the War*, Cd. 9071, Vol. XIII, p. 423.

 1928–9, *Final Report of the Committee on Industry and Trade*, Cmd. 3282, Vol. VII, p. 413.

 1929–30, *Report of the Woollen and Worsted Committee*, Cmd. 3355, Vol. XVII, p. 577.

 1931–2, *Recommendations of the Import Duties Advisory Committee and*

Additional Import Duties (No.1) Order, 1932, Cmd. 4066, Vol. XIV, p. 693.

1932–33, *Exchange of Notes between H.M. Government of the U.K. and the Government of the German Reich Regarding Commercial Relations*, Cmd. 4297, Vol. XXVII, p. 375.

1932–33, *Agreement Between the Government of the U.K. and the Government of Denmark Relating to Trade and Commerce*, Cmd. 4298, Vol. XXVII, p. 205.

1932–33, *Convention between the Government of the U.K. and the Government of the Argentine Republic Relating to Trade and Commerce*, Cmd. 4310, Vol. XXVII, p. 1.

1932–33, *Agreement between the Government of the U.K. and the Government of Sweden Relating to Trade and Commerce with Protocol and Notes Exchanged*, Cmd. 4324, Vol. XXVII, p. 811.

1932–33, *Agreement between the Government of the U.K. and the Government of Iceland Relating to Trade and Commerce, with Protocol*, Cmd. 4331, Vol. XXVII, p. 267.

1932–33, *Commerical Agreement Between the Government of the U.K. and the Government of Finland, with Protocol*, Cmd. 4425, Vol. XXVII, p. 285.

1933–34, *Commercial Agreement Between the Government of the U.K. and the Government of Finland, with Protocol*, Cmd. 4472, Vol. XXVII, p. 197.

1933–34, *Convention between the Government of the U.K. and the Government of the Argentine Republic relating to Trade and Commerce, with Protocol*, Cmd. 4492, Vol. XXVII, p. 13.

1933–34, *Agreement between H.M. Government of the U.K. and the Norwegian Government Relating to Trade and Commerce, with Protocol and Exchange of Notes*, Cmd. 4500, Vol. XXVII, p. 657.

1933–34, *Temporary Commercial Agreement Between H.M. Government and the Government of the USSR*, Cmd. 4513, Vol. XXVII, p. 759.

1933–34, *Exchange of Notes Between H.M. Government of the U.K. and the French Government Respecting Commercial Relations*, Cmd. 4590, Vol. XXVII, p. 275.

1933–34, *Agreement Between H.M. Government of the U.K. and the Government of the French Republic Relating to Trade and Commerce, with Protocol*, Cmd. 4632, Vol. XXVII, p. 279.

1933–34, *Agreement Between H.M. Government of the U.K. and the Lithuanian Government Relating to Trade and Commerce, with Protocol*, Cmd. 4648, Vol. XXVII, p. 349.

1933–34, *Agreement Between H.M. Government of the U.K. and the President of the Republic of Estonia supplementary to the Treaty of Commerce and Navigation of 18th January, 1934, with Protocol*, Cmd. 4653, Vol. XXVII, p. 149.

1934–35, *Agreement between the Government of the U.K. and the Polish Government in Regard to Trade and Commerce*, Cmd. 4820, Vol. XXIV, p. 289.

1934–35, *Provisional Agreement between H.M. Government in the U.K. and the Italian Government Regulating Imports from the U.K. into Italy*, Cmd. 4883, Vol. XXIV, p. 207.

1934-35, *Exchange of Notes Between H.M. Government in the U.K. and the Italian Government Regarding Trade and Payments*, Cmd. 4888, Vol. XXIV, p. 213.

1934-35, *Agreement Between H.M. Government in the U.K. and the Turkish Government Respecting Trade and Payments*, Cmd. 4925, Vol. XXIV, p. 469.

1934-35, *Agreement Between H.M. Government in the U.K. and the Uruguayan Government Regarding Trade and Payments*, Cmd. 4940, Vol. XXIV, p. 529.

1934-35, *Commercial Agreement Between H.M. Government in the U.K. and H.M. Government in the Union of South Africa*, Cmd. 5012, Vol. XVI, p. 719.

Brooks, Collin, *This Tariff Question* (London, E. Arnold, 1931).

Brown, A. J., 'The Fundamental Elasticities in International Trade', in T. Wilson and W. S. Andrews (eds), *Oxford Studies in the Price Mechanism* (Oxford, Clarendon Press, 1951), pp. 91–106.

Brown, A. J., 'The Present Pattern of World Trade', in *Banking and Foreign Trade* (Europa Publishers, 1952).

Brown, Benjamin H., *The Tariff Reform Movement in Great Britain, 1881–1895* (Columbia, Columbia University Press, 1943).

Brunker, E. G., *Safeguarding: What it is and What it Does* (London, Free Trade Union, 1927).

Bullock, Alan, *The Life and Times of Ernest Bevin* (London, Heinemann, 1960).

Burn, D. L., *The Economic History of Steelmaking 1867–1939* (Cambridge, Cambridge University Press, 1940).

Cairncross, A. K., 'World Trade in Manufactures Since 1900', *Economica Internazionale*, Vol. III, No.4 (1955).

Capie, Forrest, 'The British Market for Livestock Products' (PhD Thesis, London School of Economics, 1973).

Capie, Forrest, 'Consumer Preference: The Demand for Meat in England and Wales 1920–38', *Bulletin of Economic Research* Vol. 28 (1976).

Carr, J. C. and Taplin, W., *History of the British Steel Industry* (Oxford, Blackwell, 1962).

Caves, Richard E., 'Economic Models of Political Choice: Canada's Tariff Structure', *Canadian Journal of Economics*, Vol. 54 (November 1976).

Census of Production, Final Report (Board of Trade) 1924 (Third); 1930 (Fourth); 1935 (Fifth); 1948 (Sixth).

Chamberlain, Joseph, *Imperial Union and Tariff Reform* (London, G. Richards, 1903).

Chang, T. C., *Cyclical Movements in the Balance of Payments* (Cambridge, Cambridge University Press, 1951).

Chang, T. C., 'The British Balance of Payments', *Economic Journal*, Vol. 56 (1947).

Chang, T. C., 'The British Demand for Imports in the Inter-War Period', *Economic Journal*, Vol. 55 (1946) pp. 188–207.

Cheng, Hang Sheng, 'Estimates of Elasticities and Propensities in International Trade', *IMF Staff Papers*, Vols 6–7 (1960).

Clough, S. B. and Cole, C. W., *An Economic History of Europe* (Boston, D. C. Heath, 1968).

Coats, A. W., 'Political Economy and the Tariff Reform Campaign of 1903', *Journal of Law and Economics*, Vol. 11 (1968).

Coleman, D. C., *Courtaulds: An Economic and Social History, Vol. II* (London, Oxford University Press, 1969).

Comyns Carr, A. S. and Rowland Evans, D., *The Lure of Safeguarding* (London, George Allen & Unwin, 1929).

Condliffe, J. B., *The Commerce of Nations* (New York, Norton, 1950).

Cook, Chris, *The Age of Alignment Electoral Politics 1922–29* (London, Macmillan, 1975).

Corden, W. M., *The Theory of Protection* (London, Oxford University Press, 1971).

Corden, W. M., *Trade Policy and Economic Welfare* (Oxford, Clarendon Press, 1974).

Corden, W. M., 'The Costs of the Tariff', *Economic Record*, Vol. 33 (1957).

Corden, W. M., 'The Structure of a Tariff System and the Effective Protective Rate', *Journal of Political Economy*, Vol. 74 (June 1966), p. 227.

Corden, W. M. and Fels, Gerhard (eds), *Public Assistance to Industry* (London, Macmillan for Trade Policy Research Centre, 1975).

Corner, D. C., 'Exports and the British Trade Cycle: 1929', *Manchester School*, Vol. 24 (1956).

Cunningham, W., *The Case Against Free Trade* (London, J. Murray, 1911).

Customs and Excise Tariff of the United Kingdom of Great Britain and Northern Ireland (London, HMSO, January 1935).

Customs and Excise, *Imperial Preference: history and results of existing measures* (HMSO, 1929).

Daniels, G. W., 'Recent Changes in the Overseas Trade of the United Kingdom', *Transactions of the Manchester Statistical Society* (1930–31).

David, Joseph, *The World Between the Wars 1919–39* (Baltimore, Md, Johns Hopkins University Press, 1975).

Deppler, Michael C., 'Some Evidence of the Effects of Exchange Rate Changes on Trade', *IMF Staff Papers*, Vol. 21 (1974), pp. 605–36.

Devons, Ely, 'Statistics of United Kingdom Terms of Trade', *Manchester School*, Vol. 22 (September 1954).

Devons, Ely, *British Economic Statistics* (Cambridge, Cambridge University Press, 1964).

Dorrance, G. S., 'The Income Terms of Trade', *Review of Economic Studies* (1948/9).

Downs, A., *An Economic Theory of Democracy* (New York, Harper, 1957).

Drummond, Ian M., *Imperial Economic Policy, 1917–1939* (London, George Allen & Unwin, 1974).

Durbin, J. and Murphy, M. J., 'Seasonal Adjustment Based on a Mixed Additive–Multiplicative Model', *Journal of the Royal Statistical Society*, Series A, Vol. 138, Pt.3 (1975).

Eichengreen, Barry, 'The British Tariff in the 1930s' (Yale, PhD Thesis, 1981).

Eichengreen, Barry, 'The Macroeconomic Effects of the British General Tariff of 1932', Mimeograph (1979).

El-Agraa, Ali, 'On Optimum Tariffs, Retaliation, International Co-operation and Tariff Bargaining', *Bulletin of Economic Research*, Vol. 31 (1979).

Empire Industries Association Papers (London, Economic Advisory Council).

Evans, H. David, 'Effects of Protection in the General Equilibrium Framework', *Review of Economics and Statistics* Vol. 53, No.2 (1971).

Eyers, John S., 'Government Direction of Britain's Overseas Trade Policy 1932–37 (PhD Thesis, Oxford, 1977).

Falkus, M. E., 'United States Economic Policy and the "Dollar Gap" of the 1920s, *Economic History Review*, Vol. 24, No.4 (1971).

Feinstein, C. H., *Statistical Tables of National Income, Expenditure and Output of the U.K., 1855–1965* (Cambridge, Cambridge University Press, 1976).

Feldman, Gerald D., *Iron and Steel in the German Inflation 1916–1923* (Princeton, NJ, (Princeton University Press, 1977).

Findlay, R. M., *Britain under Protection* (London, George Allen & Unwin, 1935).

Foreman-Peck, J., 'Tariff Protection and Economies of Scale: The British Motor Industry before 1939', *Oxford Economic Papers*, Vol. 31 (July 1979).

Foreman-Peck, J., 'The British Tariff and Industrial Protection in the 1930s: An Alternative Model', *Economic History Review*, Vol. 34 (1981).

Francis, E. V., *Britain's Economic Strategy* (Toronto, Nelson, 1939).

Francis, F., *The Free Trade Fall* (London, J. Murray, 1926).

Free Trade Congress, *Report of the Proceedings of the International Free Trade Congress* (London, August 1908).

Friedman, Philip, *The Impact of Trade Destruction on National Incomes: A Study of Europe 1924–38* (Gainsville, University of Florida, 1974).

Geake, Charles, and Carruthers Gould, F., *John Bull's Adventures in the Fiscal Wonderland* (London, Methuen, 1904).

Glickman, David L., 'The British Imperial Preference System', *Quarterly Journal of Economics*, Vol. 61 (May 1947).

Gordon, Margaret S., *Barriers to World Trade: A Study of Recent Commercial Policy* (New York, Macmillan, 1941).

Gravil R. and Rooth, T., 'A Time of Acute Dependence: Argentina in the 1930s', *Journal of European Economic History*, Vol. 7 (1978), pp. 337–78.

Gregory, T. E., *Tariffs: A Study in Method* (London, Kelley, 1921).

Grubel, Herbert G. and Johnson, Harry, *Effective Tariff Protection* (Geneva, GATT, 1971).

Haberler, Gottfried, von, *The Theory of International Trade* (London, Wm. Hodge, 1936).

Hancock, W. K., *Survey of British Commonwealth Affairs*, Vol. II, *Problems of Economic Policy 1918–1939*, Pt.2 (Oxford, Oxford University Press, 1942).

Hannah, L., *The Rise of the Corporate Economy* (London, Methuen, 1976).

Hannah, L. and Kay, J. A., *Concentration in Modern Industry* (London, Macmillan, 1977).

Hannon Papers (House of Lords).

Harris, Seymour E., *The New Economics: Keynes' Influence on Theory and Public Policy* (London, Dobson, 1948).

Hawke, G. R., 'The United States Tariff and Industrial Protection in the Late Nineteenth Century', *Economic History Review*, Vol. 28, No.1 (1975), pp. 84–99.

Helleiner, G. K., 'The Political Economy of Canada's Tariff Structure: an Alternative Model', *Canadian Journal of Economics*, Vol. 55 (1977)

Heller, W. R., *International Trade Theory and Empirical Evidence* (New York, Prentice Hall, 1968).

Hemming, N. S. W., 'A Statistical Summary of the Extent of Import Control', *Review of Economic Studies*, Vol. 26, Pt.2, No.70 (1959).

Hewins, W. A. S., *Trade in the Balance* (London, P. Allan, 1924).

Hirschman, Albert O., *National Power and the Structure of Foreign Trade* (California, California University Bulletin of Business and Economic Research, 1945).

Hodson, H. V., 'Tariffs and Exchange Control: The Struggle to Escape', in A. J. Toynbee, *A Survey of International Affairs, 1932,* (London, Oxford University Press, 1933).

Houthaker, H. S., 'Income and Price Elasticities in World Trade', *Review of Economics and Statistics*, Vol. 2 (May 1969), pp. 111–25.

Hutchinson, Sir Herbert, *Tariff Making and Industrial Reconstruction* (London, Harrap, 1965).

Imlah, A. H. *Economic Elements in the Pax Britannica* (Cambridge, Mass., Harvard University Press, 1958).

Isserlis, L., 'Tramp Shipping Cargoes and Freights', *Journal of the Royal Statistical Society*, Pt. I (1938).

James, Robert Rhodes, *Memoirs of a Conservative: J. C. C. Davidson's Memoirs and Papers 1910–37* (London, Weidenfeld & Nicolson, 1969).

Johnson, Harry G., 'An Economic Theory of Protectionism, Tariff Bargaining and the Formation of Customs Union', *Journal of Political Economy*, Vol. 73 (1965).

Johnson, Harry G., 'Elasticity Absorption, etc.', *American Economic Review*, Vol. 66 (June 1976), pp. 445–53.

Johnson, Harry, *International Trade and Economic Growth* (London, G. Allen, 1958).

Johnson, Harry G., 'Trade Preferences and Developing Countries', *Lloyds Bank Review*, No.80 (April 1966).

Jones, J. M., *Tariff Retaliation: Repercussions of the Hawley–Smoot Bill* (Philadelphia, University of Philadelphia Press, 1934).

Kahn, Alfred E., *Great Britain in the World Economy* (New York, Columbia University Press, 1946).

Kenny, P. B., 'Problem of Seasonal Adjustment', *Statistical News* (HMSO), No.29 (May 1975).

Keynes, J. M., 'The British Balance of Trade, 1925–27', *Economic Journal*, Vol. 37 (1927), pp. 551–65.

Keynes, John Maynard, *The Economic Consequences of the Peace* (London, Macmillan, 1920).

Khan, Kishwar S., *Gains from International Trade* (Bombay, Asia Publishing House, 1971).

Kindleberger, C., *The Terms of Trade* (London, Chapman, 1956).

Kleiman, Ephraim, 'Trade and the Decline of Colonialism', *Economic Journal*, Vol. 86 (1976).

Knowles, L. C. A., *Industrial and Commercial Revolutions in Great Britain during the Nineteenth Century* (London, Routledge & Sons, 1926).

Kreinen, Mordechai, 'Disaggregated Import Demand Functions', *Southern Economic Journal*, Vol. 40 (July 1973).

Kreinen, Mordechai, 'Price Elasticities in International Trade', *Review of Economics and Statistics*, Vol. 49 (November 1967), pp. 510–16.

Kumleden, Gerhard, *The Workers' Case for Free Trade* (London, International Publishing Co., 1932).

League of Nations, *Abolition of Import and Export Prohibitions and Restrictions* (1927) Economic Committee; *The Agricultural Crisis* (1931); *Commercial Policy in the Inter-War Period* (1942); *Monthly Bulletin of Statistics*; *Statistical Yearbook* (1926–41); *World Economic Conference Final Report* (May 1927); *World Economic Survey* (1931–41); *World Production and Prices* (1925–38).

Leak, H., 'Some Results of the Import Duties Act', *Journal of the Royal Statistical Society*, Part IV (1937).

Leser, C. E. V., *Seasonality in Irish Economic Statistics*, Institute for Economic and Social Research, Paper No. 26 (Dublin, 1965)

Lewis, W. Arthur, *Economic Survey 1919–1935* (London, George Allen & Unwin, 1949).

Liepmann, H., *Tariff Levels and the Economic Unity of Europe* (London, George Allen & Unwin, 1938).

Linnemann, Hans, 'Trade Flows and Geographical Distance, or the Importance of Being Neighbours', in H. Bos (ed.), *Towards Balanced International Growth* (Amsterdam, North Holland, 1969).

LCES Annual Bulletins: Gregory, T. E., *Recent Tariff Changes* (Abroad), No. 2 (1925); Greiley, Walter, *The German Iron and Steel Industry* (1925); Delmer, A., *The Belgian Iron and Steel Industry* (1925); Jordon, R., *The French Iron and Steel Industry* (1926); Brown, F., *A Tabular Guide to the Foreign Trade Statistics of Twenty-one Principal Countries* (1926); Benham, F., *The Iron and Steel Industry of Germany, France, Belgium, Luxembourg & Saar* (1934).

McCallum, E.D., 'The Iron and Steel Industry' in *Britain in Depression* (British Association, 1935).

MacDougall, Sir Donald and Hutt, R., 'Imperial Preference: A Quantitative Analysis', *Economic Journal*, Vol. 64 (June 1954).

MacDougall, G. D. A., 'British and American Exports: a Study Suggested by Theory of Comparative Costs, Part I', *Economic Journal*, Vol. 60 (1951).

McGuire, E. B., *The British Tariff System* (London, Methuen, 1951, 2nd edn).

MacLeod, Ian, *Neville Chamberlain*, (London, S. J. R. Saunders, 1961)

Maizels, A., *Industrial Growth and World Trade* (Cambridge, Cambridge University Press, 1965).

Major, Robin, *British Trade and Exchange Rate Policy* (London, Heinemann, 1979).

Meier, Gerald M., *International Trade and Development* (New York, Harper & Row, 1963).

Meyer, F. V., *Britain's Colonies in World Trade* (Oxford, Oxford University Press, 1948).

Middlemas, Keith, *Politics in Industrial Society: the Experience of the British System since 1911* (London, Deutsch, 1979).

Minchinton, W. E., *The British Tinplate Industry* (Oxford, Oxford University Press, 1957).

Moggridge, D., *The Return to Gold, 1925* (Cambridge, Cambridge University Press, 1969).

Morrison, A. J., 'The Development of a Tariff Reform Policy during Joseph Chamberlain's First Campaign', in W. H. Challoner and Barrie M. Ratcliffe (eds), *Trade and Transport* (Manchester, Manchester University Press, 1977).

Morrison-Bell, Sir Clive, *Tariff Walls: a European Crusade* (London, J. Murray, 1930).

Morrison-Bell Papers (House of Lords).

Mowat, Charles Loch, *Britain Between the Wars 1918–40* (London, Methuen, 1968).

Murphy, M. J., *The CSO Mixed Model for Seasonal Adjustment (Brown's Method) and Model Test Programmes*, Research Exercise Note 5/73 (Central Statistical Office, 1973).

Neisser, H. and Modigliani, F., *National Incomes and International Trade* (Illinois, University of Illinois Press, 1953).

NIESR, *Trade Regulations and Commercial Policy of the United Kingdom* (Cambridge, Cambridge University Press, 1943).

Orcutt, G. H., 'Measurement of Price Elasticities in International Trade', *Review of Economic Statistics*, Vol. 32 (1950).

Page, W. T., 'Memorandum on European Bargaining Tariffs' (Geneva, League of Nations, 1927).

Parliamentary Debates, Hansard, House of Commons.

Pincus, J. J., 'Pressure Groups and the Pattern of Tariffs', *Journal of Political Economy*, Vol. 83, No. 4 (1975), p. 757.

Pincus, J. J., *Pressure Groups and Politics in Antebellum America* (New York, Columbia University Press, 1977)

Polak, J. J., *An International Economic System* (London, Allen & Unwin, 1954).

Political Economic Planning, *Report on International Trade* (London, 1937).

Pollard, Sidney, *The Development of the British Economy, 1914–1950* (London, E. Arnold, 1962).

Potter, Allen, *Organised Groups in British National Politics* (London, Faber, 1961)

Public Record Office: Board of Trade: BT 10, 11, 12, 13, 55, 56, 59, 60, 64, 90; Customs and Excise: Cust 44; Cabinet: CAB 23, 24, 27, 58; Treasury: T 160, 170, 172, 175, 177, 200.

Ramsden, John, *The Age of Balfour and Baldwin 1902–40* (London, Longman, 1978).

Reader, W. J., *Imperial Chemical Industries*, Vol. I (London, Oxford University Press, 1970).

Redmond, John, 'An Indicator of the Effective Rate of the Pound in the Nineteen Thirties', *Economic History Review*, Vol. 33, No. 1 (1980).

Richardson, H. W., *Economic Recovery in Britain, 1932–39* (London, Weidenfeld & Nicolson, 1967).

Richardson, J. Henry, *British Economic Foreign Policy* (London, Macmillan, 1936).

Richardson, J. Henry, 'Tariffs, Preferences and Other Forms of Protection', in *Britain in Recovery* (London, British Association, 1938).

Robbins, L., *The Economic Basis of Class Conflict* (London, Macmillan, 1939).

Rodwell, H. R., 'Economic Aspects of Empire Tariff Reference', *Economic Record*, Vol. 8, No.14 (1938).

Rolf, K. W. D., 'Tories, Tariffs and Elections: The West Midlands in English Politics 1918–35' (unpublished PhD Thesis, Cambridge, 1974).

Rose, Richard, *Influencing Voters: a study of campaign rationality* (London, (Faber, 1967).

Rostow, W. W., 'The Historical Analysis of the Terms of Trade', *Economic History Review*, Vol. 4 (1951).

Rostow, W. W., 'Terms of Trade in Theory and Practice', *Economic History Review*, Vol. 3 (1950).

Roth, Andrew, *The Business Background of Members of Parliament* (London, Parliamentary Profiles, 1959).

Runciman, Walter, *The Protection Menace to our Foreign Trade* (November 1930).

Salter, Sir Arthur, *Recovery* (London, G. Bell, 1933).

Saul, S. B., *Studies in British Overseas Trade 1870–1914* (Liverpool, University Press of Liverpool, 1960).

Schattschneider, E. E., *Politics, Pressure and the Tariff, A Study in Free Private Enterprise in Pressure Politics, as Shown in the 1929–30 Revision of the Tariff* (New York, Prentice Hall, 1935).

Schlote, W., *British Overseas Trade From 1700 to the 1930s* (London, Oxford University Press, 1952).

Schonfield, Hugh J. (ed.), *The Book of British Industries* (London, D. Archer, 1933).

Schuster, Sir George, 'Empire Trade before and after Ottawa', *The Economist* (3 November 1934).

Scott, M. Fg, *A Study of United Kingdom Imports* (Cambridge, Cambridge University Press, 1963).

Self, Robert, 'Tariffs and Conservative Party 1922–1931', (PhD Thesis, London School of Economics, 1980).

Shaw, Stephen, 'The Attitude of the Trades Union Congress Towards Unemployment in the Inter-War Period' (PhD Thesis, University of Kent, 1980).

Snyder, R. C., 'Commercial Policy as Reflected in Treaties from 1931–1939', *American Economic Review*, Vol. 30, No. 4. (1940).

Snyder, R. K., *The Tariff Problem in Great Britain 1918–23* (Stanford, Stanford University Press, 1944).

Statistical Abstracts for British Empire.

Statistical Abstracts for the United Kingdom (Board of Trade, HMSO).

Stern, R. M., Francis, J. and Schumaster, B., *Price Elasticities in International Trade* (London, Macmillan, 1976).

Sundararajan, V., 'The Impact of the Tariff on Some Selected Products of the U.S. Iron and Steel Industry 1870–1914, *Quarterly Journal of Economics*, Vol. 84 (November 1970), pp. 590–610.

Sykes, Alan, *Tariff Reform in British Politics 1903–1913* (Oxford, Oxford University Press, 1979).

Tariff Commission: *Abandonment of Cobdenism* (1913); *Industrial Crisis and British Policy* (1921); *Trade Crisis and the Remedy* (1922); *The Tariff Policy: how it works* (1932); *The War and British Economic Policy.* (1915).

Taussig, F. W., *Principles of Economics* (New York, Macmillan, 1930).

Taussig, F. W., 'The Change in Great Britain's Foreign Trade Terms after 1900', *Economic Journal*, Vol. 34 (1925).

Taylor, A. J. P., *English History 1914–45* (Oxford, Clarendon Press, 1965).

Thackeray, F. G., 'Elasticity of Demand for United Kingdom Imports', *Bulletin of the Oxford University Institute of Statistics*, Vol. 12, No. 4 (April 1950), pp. 109–14.

Thirlwall, A. P., 'Trends and Cycles in Import Penetration in the United Kingdom', *Oxford Bulletin of Economics and Statistics*, Vol. 39 (November 1977).

Tomlinson, J. D., 'Anglo-Indian Economic Relations, 1913–1928, with special reference to the cotton trade' (PhD Thesis, London School of Economics, 1977).

Trade and Navigation Accounts (see *Accounts Relating to the Trade and Navigation of the United Kingdom*)

Trades Union Congress, General Council of Economic Committee, *Tariffs & World Trade: an Examination of our fiscal policy* (London, 1932).

Traves, Tom, *The State and Enterprise: Canadian Manufacturers and the Federal Government, 1917–1931* (Toronto, University of Toronto Press, 1979).

Triantis, S. G., *Cyclical Changes in Trade Balances of Countries Exporting*

Primary Products 1927–33, (Toronto, Canadian Association for Adult Education, 1967)

Turner, John, 'The British Commonwealth Union and the General Election of 1918', *English Historical Review*, Vol. 93 (July 1978).

Vaizey, John, *The History of British Steel* (London, Weidenfeld & Nicolson, 1974).

Viner, J., *Dumping: A Problem in International Trade* (Chicago, Chicago University Press, 1923).

Viner, J., 'Economic Thought: Mercantilist Thought', *International Encyclopaedia of the Social Sciences*, Vol. 4 (1934), pp. 435–43.

Viner, J., *Studies in the Theory of International Trade* (New York, Harper, 1937).

Vogel, Robert, *A Breviate of British Diplomatic Blue Books 1919–1939* (Montreal, McGill University Press, 1963).

Walker, Ronald, *Why Tariffs Have Failed* (London, Dickson, 1934).

Williams, Herbert G., *Through Tariffs to Prosperity* (London, P. Allan, 1931).

Williams, L. J., *Britain and the World Economy 1919–1970* (London, Fontana, 1971).

Winch, Donald, *Economics and Policy* (London, Hodder & Stoughton, 1969).

Yates, P. Lamartine, *Forty Years of Foreign Trade* (London, Allen & Unwin, 1959).

Yeager, Leland B. and Tuerck, David G., *Foreign Trade and U.S. Policy* (New York, Praeger, 1976).

Zelder, Raymond E., 'Estimates of Elasticities of Demand for Exports of the United Kingdom and the United States 1921–1938', *Manchester School*, No. 1 (1958).

Index